FOOTBALL NOW!

FOOTBALL NOW!

SECOND EDITION

MIKE LEONETTI
and JOHN IABONI

FIREFLY BOOKS

A FIREFLY BOOK

Published by Firefly Books Ltd. 2009

First printing

Publisher Cataloging-in-Publication Data (U.S.)
Leonetti, Mike, 1958-
    Football now / Mike Leonetti and John Iaboni.
2nd ed.
[   ] p. : col. ill., col. ports. ;   cm.
Includes index.
Summary: Profiles of eighty-six National Football League players.
ISBN-13: 978-1-55407-449-5 (pbk.)
ISBN-10: 1-55407-449-5 (pbk.)
1. National Football League -- Biography. 2. Football players --United States
-- Biography. I. Iaboni, John. II. Title.
796.332/64092273 dc22   GV939 A1L455 2009

Library and Archives Canada Cataloguing in Publication
Leonetti, Mike, 1958-
    Football now! / Mike Leonetti and John Iaboni. -- 2nd ed.
Includes index.
ISBN-13: 978-1-55407-449-5
ISBN-10: 1-55407-449-5
    1. Football players--United States--Biography. 2. National Football
League--Biography. 3. Football players--United States--Pictorial works.
4. National Football League--Pictorial works.
I. Iaboni, John II. Title.

GV939.A1 L45 2009   796.332'64092273   C2009-900764-9

Published in the United States by
Firefly Books (U.S.) Inc.
P.O. Box 1338, Ellicott Station
Buffalo, New York 14205

Published in Canada by
Firefly Books Ltd.
66 Leek Crescent
Richmond Hill, Ontario L4B 1H1

Cover and interior design: Luna Design

Printed in China

The publisher gratefully acknowledges the financial support for our
publishing program by the Government of Canada through the Book
Publishing Industry Development Program.

PHOTO CREDITS

Getty Images

Bill Baptist 99; Al Bello 109, 150, 151,
153; Doug Benc 22, 33, 43, 51, 154,
176; Scott Boehm 13, 23, 45, 52, 53, 61,
78, 147, 152; Rex Brown 85, 106, 107;
Domenic Centofanti 175; Timothy A.
Clary 6; Kevin C. Cox 12, 89, 95; Scott
Cunningham 120, 121, 155; Tom Dahlin
2, 21, 36, 70, 71; Stephen Dunn 90, 110;
Elsa 15, 97; Jonathan Ferrey 16; Larry
French 50; George Gojkovich 126, 127;
Chris Graythen 29, 80; Sam Greenwood
56; Otto Greule Jr 174; Drew Hallowell
27, 31, 60, 81, 166; T. Hauck 24, 25, 113,
139; Wesley Hitt 34, 103; Paul Jasienski
117, 122, 164; Streeter Lecka 63, 94,
112, 169; Ben Liebenberg 88; G Newman
Lowrance 93, 111, 129, 146, 163; Andy
Lyons 10, 67, 74, 75, 96; Hunter Martin
44, 167; Ronald Martinez 98, 100, 116,
156, 171; Larry Maurer 58; Jim McIsaac
14, 38, 48; Al Messerschmidt 20, 26;
Donald Miralle 3, 11, 76, 77; Ronald C.
Modra/Sports 165; Peter Newcomb 86;
Doug Pensinger 18, 37; Evan Pinkus 30,
143; Joe Robbins 8–9, 17, 39, 40, 46–47,
68, 69, 72, 82, 84, 115, 118–119, 128,
132, 148, 149, 157, 160–161, 168, 173;
Jim Rogash 19, 105; Eliot J. Schechter 32;
Gregory Shamus 41, 108, 170, 172; Paul
Spinelli 35, 55, 66, 131, 133, 134; Jamie
Squire 57, 102; Rick Stewart 130; David
Stluka 124, 144–145; Matthew Stockman
7, 79; Kevin Terrell 28, 42, 142; Rob
Tringali/Sportschrome 64, 65, 73, 87, 123,
125, 136–137, 158; Greg Trott 54, 104,
114, 135, 140, 159, 162; Tim Umphrey
62, 141; Dilip Vishwanat 59, 92, 138;
Thomas E. White 91

Front cover: Kevin C. Cox (Larry
Fitzgerald); Jim McIsaac (Troy Polamalu);
Joe Robbins (Peyton Manning); Kevin
Terrell (Adrian Peterson); Greg Trott
(Randy Moss)

Back Cover: Al Bello (Ray Lewis); Jim
McIsaac (Marion Barber); Joe Robbins
(Ben Roethlisberger)

*The authors would like to dedicate this book
to football fans everywhere …
through good times and bad, they cheer and support
the NFL from Kickoff Weekend in autumn
until Super Bowl Sunday in winter.*

Contents

Introduction

Football Now! is the story of how during a complex time, some things never change. Playing NFL football can be financially rewarding, but you can't buy a championship. Winning a Super Bowl is still defined by the principles of hard work, discipline and sportsmanship. That was proved by the 2008 Pittsburgh Steelers, who romped their way to an unprecedented sixth Super Bowl victory, the second in four years, with timely offense and the league's best defense — the Steel Curtain reborn!

The march to six NFL titles in Pittsburgh has been orchestrated by coaching legends the likes of Chuck Noll and Bill Cowher, and now the fresh-faced Mike Tomlin, who at 36 became the youngest coach ever to win the Lombardi Trophy. His era is one not defined by chalkboard plays and X's and O's, but by high-tech tools that instantly provide benches with snapshots of plays that happened only seconds before. For Tomlin, and all those who have come before him and those who will follow in his footsteps, instilling his team with the will to win is, and always will be, the hardest part of the job.

Football Now! is the story of aging superstars showing their magic once more, like Tony Gonzalez, Hines Ward and Kurt Warner, and a new wave of stars whose time has arrived, such as Adrian Peterson, Larry Fitzgerald and Matt Ryan. Covered in these pages are stories about great plays and misplays, euphoria and dejection, blessed lives and troubled times; there are more than a few NFLers who have had to cast aside tough upbringings, and many who are having to deal with current off-field problems. Some overcome their difficulties while others are consumed by them. Sometimes, ultimately, the law is the agent that disciplines players, a troubling aspect of a league that is trying hard to ensure its role models are a positive influence on young fans.

Football Now! is the story of the fan. The in-game experience, whether live or through the media, is all encompassing: instant replays, analysis and camera angles covering every inch of the field are offered to observers at every moment. Today the NFL fan can be brought right into the huddle and can follow the ball from every conceivable angle, while capturing every crunching sound. It is the opportunity for every fan to be part of the stadium atmosphere without even being there!

In 2008, the NFL's marketing slogan was "Believe in Now," a sentiment echoed throughout the pages of *Football Now!* Today's NFL is packed with more capable superstars at every position than ever before. What follows is a glimpse into the story of *Football Now!* — the careers of the 86 most influential players currently thrilling the football world.

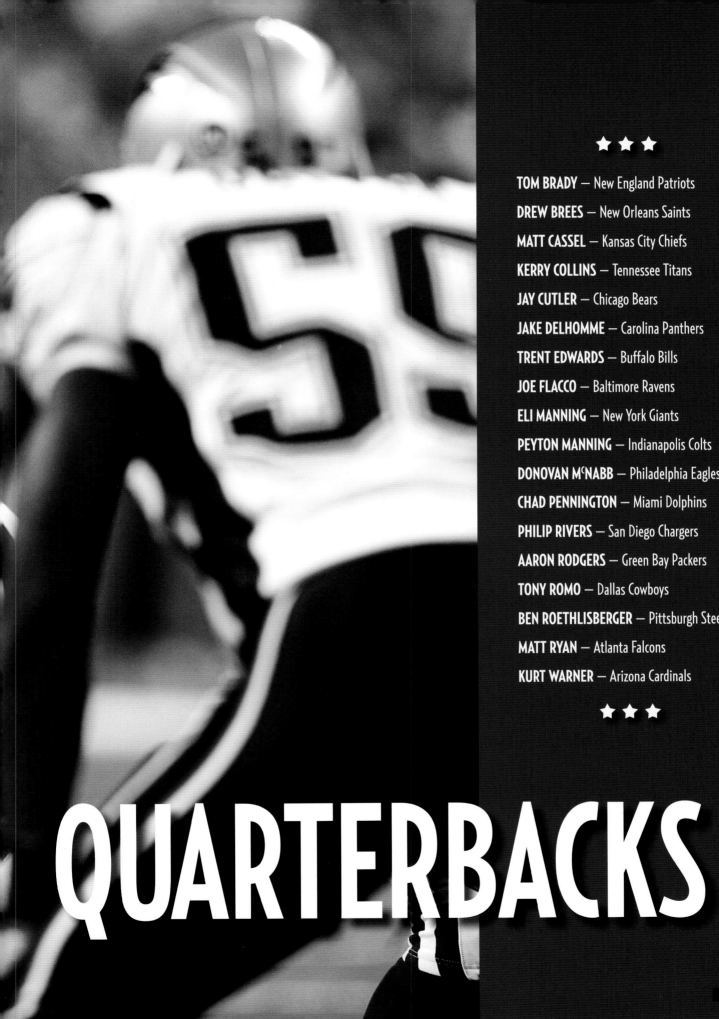

TOM BRADY — New England Patriots

DREW BREES — New Orleans Saints

MATT CASSEL — Kansas City Chiefs

KERRY COLLINS — Tennessee Titans

JAY CUTLER — Chicago Bears

JAKE DELHOMME — Carolina Panthers

TRENT EDWARDS — Buffalo Bills

JOE FLACCO — Baltimore Ravens

ELI MANNING — New York Giants

PEYTON MANNING — Indianapolis Colts

DONOVAN M^cNABB — Philadelphia Eagles

CHAD PENNINGTON — Miami Dolphins

PHILIP RIVERS — San Diego Chargers

AARON RODGERS — Green Bay Packers

TONY ROMO — Dallas Cowboys

BEN ROETHLISBERGER — Pittsburgh Steelers

MATT RYAN — Atlanta Falcons

KURT WARNER — Arizona Cardinals

QUARTERBACKS

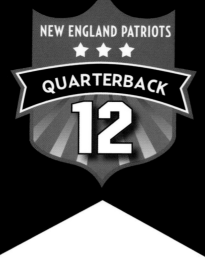

NEW ENGLAND PATRIOTS
★ ★ ★

QUARTERBACK

12

TOM BRADY

CAREER HIGHLIGHTS

• Named NFL MVP in 2007.

• Broke Peyton Manning's single-season record of 49 touchdowns, set in 2004, with 50 in 2007.

• Named to four Pro Bowls (2001, 2004, 2005, 2007).

It happened so suddenly, no one had time to contemplate the fact New England Patriots star quarterback Tom Brady might be injured so badly. As Brady dropped back to pass in the opening game of the 2008 season, Kansas City safety Bernard Pollard fell on his leg, bending the limb in an awkward way. Brady was tended to on the field, but managed to walk to the dressing room on his own. Any hopes he was not seriously injured quickly evaporated, however, when the Patriots announced he would be out for the rest of the season. New England, as per team policy, does not reveal the exact nature of injuries, but it was widely speculated Brady tore the ACL and MCL in his left knee. Surgery was required to repair the ligaments. Then it was reported an infection had set in, which meant doctors had to go back and make further adjustments. While not happy about missing an entire season, Brady quickly re-focused and did his best to keep positive thoughts. As 2009 began, Brady stated rehabilitation of the knee was moving along as anticipated and that he would be participating in all the pre-season training requirements.

The hope upon Brady's return to the NFL will be that one of the great careers in league history will pick up right where it left off. He won his first three Super Bowl trips with the Patriots following the 2001, 2003 and 2004 seasons, claiming the game MVP award on two occasions. He took his team to the championship game once more after an incredible undefeated 2007 season, but lost to the New York Giants on the big stage. That spoiled the Pats' chance to join the 1972 Miami Dolphins as the only teams to end an entire NFL season without a loss.

Brady started his NFL career in 2001 when former Patriots quarterback Drew Bledsoe was injured and Brady set a league record by throwing his first 162 passes with no interceptions. The 6-foot-5, 225-pound quarterback has thrown for over 26,000 yards to date to go along with 197 touchdowns. His numbers are astonishing considering Brady was selected 199th overall in 2000.

IN THE HUDDLE
Brady was drafted in the 18th round of the 1995 MLB draft by the Montreal Expos as a back catcher.

As great as Brady has been, his replacement, Matt Cassel, won 11 games in 2008, although the Patriots missed the playoffs. It's a nice problem in one way to have two capable pivots, but salary

cap implications meant one of them had to be moved. The big question facing New England, assuming Brady was healthy, was who would stay and who would be traded away. Most football experts thought the Patriots would bring both players to training camp before making such an important decision, but they did not wait that long. A deal was consummated with Kansas City that saw Cassel and veteran linebacker Mike Vrabel shipped to the Chiefs in exchange for a second round draft choice. While the trade may have been a surprise to some, those familiar with how the Patriots operate were not so shocked. The organization is generally very loyal to those who have performed well for them. For example, recall how they let linebacker Tedy Bruschi recover from a serious heart problem and then inserted him back in their lineup without any hesitation. No one has performed better than Brady, though the Patriots also have high hopes for 6-foot-5, 225-pound quarterback Kevin O'Connell, a native of Knoxville, Tennessee who was drafted in the third round of the 2008 NFL draft.

Such faith in his ability to recover must give Brady some confidence as he regains his starting job. It will be easier to do so without having to answer questions about Cassel and what he did for the Patriots while Brady was out. Brady also comes to a new season as a married man after his wedding to 28-year-old Brazilian supermodel Gisele Bundchen. They were married at St. Monica Catholic Church in the Los Angeles suburb of Santa Monica, an oceanfront community, in front of mostly immediate family members. In case the 31-year-old Brady's career should end prematurely, he does not have to worry about money since his new wife reportedly earns roughly $35 million a year. Such security should give Brady plenty of peace of mind as he takes to the field to resume his career.

DREW BREES

NEW ORLEANS SAINTS
★ ★ ★
QUARTERBACK
9

It took quarterback Drew Brees three years to get the San Diego Chargers into the playoffs after he became the team's starter in 2002. The Bolts selected Brees after his career at Purdue University ended with a Rose Bowl loss to the Washington Huskies, marking it the first time the Boilermakers had played in the game since 1967.

The Chargers were an awful 1–15 in the season leading up to the 2001 draft. Because of that, they selected running back LaDainian Tomlinson first overall, then took Brees with the 32nd pick. They immediately slotted Brees behind starter Doug Flutie for the 2001 regular season, but named him the starter for the 2002 campaign. A solid year of 8–8 was followed by a bad one at 4–12, but then Brees started to find his game. He took his team to a 12–4 mark in 2004 and a spot in the playoffs. A loss to the Jets ended San Diego's hopes and the next season was a bit of nightmare that saw Brees sustain a serious shoulder injury in the last game of the year. The Chargers forgot all about Brees' efforts to make them respectable and let him become a free agent. The New Orleans Saints are still very grateful for that decision.

Many people were quick to criticize the Saints for signing Brees because of his surgically repaired shoulder and the fact he was not the biggest quarterback out there at an even 6-foot and 209 pounds. Residents of New Orleans were looking for something positive coming off the ravaging of their city by Hurricane Katrina and the football team was a symbol of hope for many. Brees said and did all the right things, like buying a house in an area that had been badly hit during the hurricane, and then went out and gave the Saints their best year ever. New Orleans won the NFC South Division with a 10–6 record and

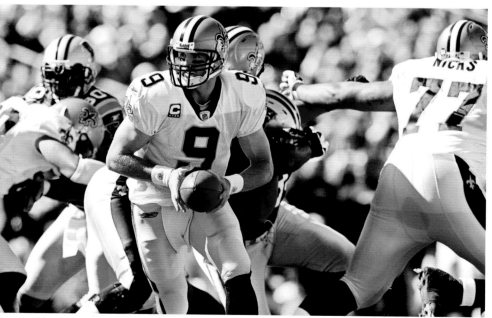

CAREER HIGHLIGHTS

- Drafted 32nd overall from Purdue University by the San Diego Chargers in 2001.

- Named the 2008 Associated Press offensive player of the year.

- Only the second person in NFL history to pass for over 5,000 yards in a season (5,069 yards in 2008).

- Selected to three Pro Bowls (2004, 2006, 2008).

Brees was simply outstanding with 4,418 passing yards and 440 pass completions, 26 of them touchdowns. The Saints won their home playoff game against the Philadelphia Eagles 27–24 and that got them a spot in the NFC title game against Chicago. New Orleans could never get going in cold Soldier Field, falling behind early and going on to lose 39–14. The Saints came up a little short of the Super Bowl, but a team and a quarterback had won the hearts of a city, state and maybe even the country.

IN THE HUDDLE

In the 2007 regular season, Drew Brees set the NFL single-season record for most passes completed with 440.

While a 7–9 season in 2007 was a disappointment for everyone in New Orleans, Brees was one of the few bright spots by once again passing for over 4,000 yards. In 2008, Brees' performance was even more impressive. He finished with 5,069 passing yards, a mere 16 yards short of the NFL record held by former Miami Dolphin Dan Marino. It marked only the second time a quarterback exceeded the 5,000-yard mark and all of his teammates were upset Brees did not set a new standard. But the pivot himself was more concerned that the team was only a mediocre 8–8 and once again out of the playoffs. He was named the Associated Press offensive player of the year, earning the award ahead of NFL MVP Peyton Manning and star running back Adrian Peterson. (Ironically, Brees shared the league lead for touchdowns (34) with his replacement in San Diego, Philip Rivers.) Another 2008 highlight for Brees was beating his old team 37–32 in a regular season game played in London, England.

Brees is one of the hardest-working players in the NFL. He likes to be involved in all the strategy meetings and even opposing coaches have noted how well Brees can read a play before it develops. He meshes very well with head coach Gary Payton, who has complete faith in his on-field general. New Orleans endured many injuries to key offensive players, and at one point late in the season 11 different Saints had caught passes from Brees for touchdowns.

Brees has turned 30, but still has prime years ahead of him. His career numbers will only be enhanced the longer he plays and they may one day make him worthy of Hall of Fame consideration. The Saints have never been to the Super Bowl and if anybody can lead them there, it's Brees.

MATT CASSEL

The New England Patriots have a well-deserved reputation for keeping all their scouting information a tightly guarded secret. Based on how many gems they've culled from the draft, you can bet every team would love a glimpse at the Pats' notes. The team is also known for really listening to their scouts; knowing their opinion is valued makes the birddogs feel all the more important. Scouting is a largely thankless job and only a few make it up the ranks to gain higher positions in the league, but it remains a vital function for every professional sports team. Matt Russell was a scout based on the West Coast for New England and a former NFL linebacker with the Detroit Lions. He recommended the Patriots consider drafting quarterback Matt Cassel out of USC despite the fact the pivot had not started a single game in college.

IN THE HUDDLE

Cassel is the only player in NFL history to start in an NFL game without ever getting a start in college.

Cassel had good size at 6-foot-4 and 230 pounds, but all he ever did at USC was backup more prominent quarterbacks and future NFLers like Carson Palmer and Matt Linehart. He tried hard to impress on special teams or whatever role he was called upon to perform. New England asks that their scouts assess each player who is going to graduate — even those who might not play very much — especially if they play in a major program. It's a good strategy and Russell was asked to look at Cassel closely during practice by a USC coach. Afterward, the scout made his first contact with the Patriots front office about what he had seen after being very impressed with the way the youngster tossed the ball. On another occasion, Russell and other NFL scouts were asked to look at Cassel and everyone liked what they saw, meaning there might be some competition for the quarterback after all. Many believed Cassel would be a free agent signing after the 2005 NFL draft, but Russell implored Pats vice-president Scott Pioli and coach Bill Belichick to spend a draft choice on what he thought was a talented quarterback. Using the 230th pick of the draft in the seventh round, the Patriots complied with their scout and selected Cassel.

The mere drafting of Cassel might have been the end of the story, but he made the team in 2005. For the next three seasons, Cassel served as a backup to one of the best quarterbacks ever in

Tom Brady, a three-time Super Bowl winner. However, all that changed when Brady badly injured a knee in the opening game of the 2008 season and was forced to miss the rest of the year. Suddenly Cassel, who had never started a single NFL contest and had thrown all of 39 passes, was the starter for a team expected to go back to the Super Bowl to avenge its upset loss to the New York Giants. Most pundits felt the season was over for New England, but they didn't know the Patriots had a secret weapon on their bench just waiting to get a chance.

By the time the 2008 season was over the Patriots had posted an 11–5 mark, but lost the division lead in the tie-breaker formula to the Miami Dolphins (who had the same win-loss record) and finished out of the playoffs. Cassel put up more than respectable numbers by throwing 21 touchdowns (giving up only 11 interceptions) while completing 63.4 percent of his passes. He was good from the moment he replaced Brady in the opening game, guiding the team to a 17–10 victory over Kansas City, and put together back-to-back 400-yard passing games over Miami and the New York Jets in November. Belichick noted Cassel was a very hard worker who was very committed to doing his best. The head coach felt his replacement quarterback had performed impressively throughout the '08 campaign — great praise from a very demanding and successful coach.

Cassel's salary in 2008 was a mere $520,000, but when the Patriots gave him the franchise player designation (a one-year option to protect a franchise caliber player from the free-agency market), it automatically meant Cassel would earn the average salary of the top five quarterbacks in the league, or $14.6 million in 2009. Cassel quickly accepted the one-year offer. With Brady still in the fold and his recovery on schedule, New England opted to trade Cassel to Kansas City as opposed to having two quarterbacks on the payroll at a total of $29 million. Cassel will now be a key figure in the Chiefs' bid to rebuild their franchise.

CAREER HIGHLIGHTS

• Backed up former Heisman Trophy winners Carson Palmer and Matt Leinart.

• Was the most sacked quarterback in 2008 taking 47 sacks.

• Was the first player since 1970 to throw for 400 yards and rush for 60 yards in the same game when he did so on November 13 against the New York Jets.

• Was named the AFC offensive player of the week in Week 12.

• Cassel's No.16 that he wore in New England has been retired by Kansas City in honor of quarterback Len Dawson; Cassel will wear No.7 instead.

KERRY COLLINS

Of all the completions quarterback Kerry Collins has made, one that occurred off the field was his most important. His demon was a battle with alcoholism that, at its height, led to him utter a racial epithet to a teammate in what he thought was a joking manner in 1997 and an arrest in 1998 for driving under the influence.

Collins sought treatment with humility and commitment. The recovery then permitted Kerry Michael Collins to concentrate on the aspects that matter most: his family, community-minded initiatives where he's renowned for his kindness and running offenses.

One of "Papa" Joe Paterno's prized protégés at Penn State, Collins first tossed a pass in the NFL with the Carolina Panthers in 1995. His career path then took him to the New Orleans Saints (1998), the New York Giants (1999), the Oakland Raiders (2004) and the Tennessee Titans (2006).

Coming off the 2007 season where Collins started just one of the six games he played, the graybeard was the backup when the Titans faced the Jacksonville Jaguars in Week 1 of 2008. But when Vince Young injured his left leg with 4:14 to play, in came Collins. His first play was a third-and-15 situation at the Titans 30 and he connected with tight end Bo Scaife for a 44-yard screen play.

IN THE HUDDLE
Collins was the first draft pick in Carolina Panthers team history.

LenDale White then rushed for six before losing two. Staring at third and six from the Jags 22, Collins combined with wideout Justin Gage for a 21-yard gain. White followed by crashing over from the one. Tennessee moved ahead 17–10 and held on for the first of 10 consecutive wins. Collins started the next 15 games for the Titans, who finished 13–3 for the best record in the NFL. He even played a solid game in the divisional playoffs against the Baltimore Ravens with 26 completions in 42 attempts for 281 yards. But miscues, including a Collins interception, kept the Ravens alive and they eventually won 13–10.

Born on December 30, 1972 in Lebanon, Pennsylvania, the 6-foot-5, 245-pound pivot did his part in maintaining Penn State's winning tradition. He steered the Nittany Lions to wins in his final 17 starts, including a 12–0 mark in 1994 that culminated with a 38–20 win over Oregon in the Rose Bowl. At

Wilson High School in West Lawn, Pennsylvania, his success wasn't confined to football. He was a noted center in basketball and pitcher in baseball. In fact, two Major League Baseball teams drafted Collins — the Detroit Tigers in 1990 (26th round) and the Toronto Blue Jays in 1994 (58th round).

The 1995 NFL draft reflected the stature Penn State possessed as running back Ki-Jana Carter went first overall to the Cincinnati Bengals while Collins went No. 5 — the first-ever collegiate player drafted by expansion Carolina. Penn State tight end Kyle Brady also went in the top 10 at No. 9 to the New York Jets.

The Panthers finished a respectable 7–9 in Year 1. Collins had taken over as No. 1 QB in Week 4 and guided them to a 7–6 record after the 0–3 start. The Panthers clawed their way to the NFC championship in Year 2, where they lost to the Green Bay Packers.

But five games into 1998, Collins was waived by the Panthers and picked up by the Saints. With the off-field issues taking their toll, Collins went about rebuilding himself and in the process he latched on with the Giants. From backup, he became starter in seven of the 10 games he played in 1999, including the final six contests. He started 67 games in a row for the Giants before an injury kayoed him for the final three games of 2003. The following season, Kurt Warner and Eli Manning were with the Giants and Collins became a Raider, first as the backup to Rich Gannon and then starter for the final 13 games of 2004 and 15 games in 2005.

Collins signed with the Titans in 2006 as the No. 1 QB, but after three consecutive losses, Vince Young stepped in. Collins always kept the No. 1 mentality and was ready when head coach Jeff Fisher sent him in early in 2008. He completed 242

CAREER HIGHLIGHTS

- Two-time Pro Bowl selection (1996, 2008).
- Tied for the NFL record for fumbles in a season with 23 in 2001.
- Is the NFL's second-leading active passer.
- During his senior season at Penn State Collins won the Davey O'Brien Award for top college quarterback in the NCAA and the Maxwell Award for the nation's most outstanding player.

of 415 passes for 2,676 yards with 12 TDs and seven interceptions in 2008, when he also gained his second trip to the Pro Bowl.

He made it clear he wasn't quite ready to retire to his 1,580-acre ranch in Asheboro, North Carolina, just yet.

JAY CUTLER

The Denver Broncos opened the 2008 NFL season by beating the Oakland Raiders 41–14, but it looked like they were about to lose the second contest of the year to the San Diego Chargers. Denver was driving for the winning points when quarterback Jay Cutler fumbled the ball on a pass attempt and it was recovered by San Diego. The referee made the wrong call — ruling the ball had actually not been fumbled — and gave it back to the Broncos. Given a second life, Cutler hit receiver Eddie Royal for a four-yard touchdown and then found Royal again for a two-point conversion that gave Denver a thrilling 39–38 victory.

As the final moments played out, Cutler looked more and more like former Bronco legend John Elway, completing 36 of 50 passes for 341 yards and then very coolly making deadly accurate throws with the game on the line. Cutler led Denver to four wins in its first five games in 2008 and a trip to the playoffs seemed inevitable. It looked like Cutler was going to elevate his team to elite status, just as Elway had done for many of his years as Broncos QB.

It was inevitable the 6-foot-3, 233-pound Cutler would be compared to Elway, Denver's franchise-defining player and a two-time Super Bowl winner. Actually, Cutler has many similarities to Elway — they're about the same size and both were very good baseball players in high school. Elway was a standout quarterback at Stanford, while Cutler racked up great numbers at Vanderbilt. And each, of course, was a high draft pick, with Cutler selected 11th overall in 2006, while Elway went No. 1 overall in 1983. Their respective careers did not overlap in Denver, but each was firmly entrenched as the Broncos starter before they hit their 25th birthday. It was more difficult for Cutler since he was following a legend, but he managed to make his own mark on the team and league.

IN THE HUDDLE
Jay Cutler's 4,526 passing yards in 2008 as a member of the Denver Broncos broke Jake Plummer's single-season team record of 4,089 that was set in 2004.

Cutler started the last five games of his rookie year in 2006 and kept the job for the start of the 2007 season. Prior to that campaign, Cutler was diagnosed with Type I diabetes. Finding out he had the disease was a complete shock to him and Cutler lost 35 pounds. He put the weight back on after he started taking insulin injections and adjusted his diet appropriately. In spite of his condition he threw for 3,497 yards and 20 touchdowns, but Denver only finished with a 7–9 record. He came back with a very strong performance in 2008 by throwing for a club-record 4,526 yards and 25 touchdowns, though he was also picked off 18 times. The Broncos wanted to emulate the New England Patriots offense and relied on the strong-armed Cutler to lead the way. Cutler was trusted to hold onto the ball longer and look

CAREER HIGHLIGHTS

- Cutler received first-team all-state honors as a senior in high school, leading his school, Heritage Hills High School in Lincoln City, Indiana, to a 15–0 record and its first state title; he was named a first-team all-state selection in basketball while garnering an all-state honourable mention as a baseball shortstop.

- Selected to his first Pro Bowl in 2008.

- Became the first Bronco to begin his career by throwing a touchdown pass in each of his first nine games.

for big plays down field instead of settling for shorter, safer completions that would only serve to pad the quarterback's statistics. He made 616 throws and completed 384 passes as Denver tried to cover for a very leaky defense. The Broncos surrounded Cutler with a good supporting group of players on offense that included receivers like Royal and Brandon Marshall, a solid tight end in Tony Scheffler and a rookie left tackle in Ryan Clady, who was able to protect the quarterback's blind side.

In spite of their new approach to attacking, the Broncos ran into trouble after the first five games of the season and finished a mediocre 8–8. They lost the division title to San Diego on the last night of the season, getting whipped 52–21 by the Chargers. It was the third straight loss for the Broncos and it cost a very good coach, Mike Shanahan, his job. Cutler was once again denied a chance to play a post-season game, something he has not done

since high school.

In the off-season the Broncos named Josh McDaniels as their new head coach and discussions were held with New England about acquiring Matt Cassel, a quarterback McDaniels had coached with the Patroits. Cassel eventually went to Kansas City but Cutler was highly offended such talks were ever held and asked for a trade. McDaniels attempts at reconciliation with Cutler were fruitless, essentially forcing Denver to trade their starting pivot. A deal was worked out with the Chicago Bears that saw Cutler and a 2009 fifth-round pick go to the Windy City while the Broncos received two first-round draft picks (2009, 2010) a 2009 third-round pick and quarterback Kyle Orton.

Cutler was thrilled to be sent to a team he grew up cheering for, and the Bears immediately helped him out by signing seven time Pro Bowl offensive tackle Orlando Pace to protect their newest saviour.

JAKE DELHOMME

When the Carolina Panthers launched into 2008, there was a feeling all was right once more at the quarterback position. Jake Delhomme was back, throwing harder passes as accurately as ever.

The longtime Panthers starter had Carolina off to a 2–1 start in 2007 when things came to a crashing halt with season-ending surgery on his right elbow. Minus Delhomme, the Panthers tumbled to a record of 7–9.

Delhomme's return couldn't have been choreographed any better. Even with his good friend and favorite target Steve Smith out with a two-game, team-imposed suspension, Delhomme

produced a magical finish in Week 1 of 2008. Starting on his own 32-yard line with 2:21 to play and the Panthers down 24–19 at San Diego, Delhomme worked a perfect two-minute drill.

On the game's final play with two seconds to go, he took the snap and fired a perfect pass to tight end Dante Rosario for a 14-yard touchdown. Delhomme then went berserk with excitement. That wasn't the first time his dramatics produced a wildly exciting win for Carolina. Basically, his flair for miracle finishes earned him the No. 1 spot with the Panthers in the first place.

Week 1 of 2003 was when that happened. With Rodney Peete at the helm and designated as the starter for the season, the Panthers trailed 17–0 at the half against the Jacksonville Jaguars. In came Delhomme, who clicked for three TD passes in what became a 24–23 win. He was installed as the starter and Carolina steamrolled to a 5–0 start. The Panthers finished 11–5 on the season and won the NFC championship by defeating Dallas (29–10), St. Louis (29–23) and Philadelphia (14–3). Their dream season didn't end until Adam Vinatieri's 41-yard field goal with four seconds to play gave New England the

CAREER HIGHLIGHTS
- Selected to play the Pro Bowl in 2005.
- Was the only true freshman quarterback to start for a Division 1A school in 1993, when he started for the University of Louisiana-Lafayette.
- Went undrafted in the 1997 NFL Draft, signed as a free agent with the New Orleans Saints.

32–29 triumph in Super Bowl XXXVIII.

Delhomme is of Cajun stock, born in Lafayette, Louisiana, on January 10, 1975. From an early age, he gained a love of horses because his grandfather, Sanders, was a horse breeder while his father, Jerry, was a jockey at a young age. That passion continues today as Delhomme, his father and brother, Jeff, are partners in a group that purchases and trains thoroughbreds in Louisiana.

At Teurlings Catholic High School in Lafayette, Delhomme was a QB and defensive back. He maintained his star status at college with the Louisiana-Lafayette Ragin' Cajuns, but even with a senior year that included 2,901 yards passing and 20 touchdowns, he went undrafted.

IN THE HUDDLE

Delhomme's passer rating of 113.6 was the highest for a quarterback starting his first Super Bowl since Steve Young posted a passer rating of 134.8 in Super Bowl XXIX.

New Orleans offered some NFL hope for the 6-foot-2, 215-pounder and he spent 1998 on the Saints practice roster. A year later, he was backing up Kurt Warner with Europe's Amsterdam Admirals before serving as third QB on the Saints depth chart. In 1999, he steered the Frankfurt Galaxy to the World Bowl Championship before reporting back to New Orleans, where he actually got into two NFL games and won his first start with a two-TD passing performance against Dallas.

A spare part in New Orleans, Delhomme tested free agency in 2003 and chose the Panthers over the Cowboys. The move was an astute one by both Delhomme and the Panthers as their union clicked. In 2005, Delhomme made it to the Pro Bowl after his third consecutive season of passing for more than 3,200 yards.

Following his injury in 2007, Delhomme put up 3,288 yards passing in 2008 with 15 TDs and 12 interceptions. The Panthers sealed the No. 2 seed in the NFC with a record of 12–4.

But Carolina met disappointment after a 33–13 playoff loss on home turf to Warner's Arizona Cardinals. It was a miserable day for the Panthers and especially Delhomme, who was celebrating his 34th birthday. He was picked off five times — one away from tying the NFL post-season record — and coughed up a fumble. Rich Gannon of the Oakland Raiders was the last QB to have five passes intercepted in the playoffs, his awful game coming in the 48–21 loss to the Tampa Bay Buccaneers in Super Bowl XXXVII.

For Delhomme, the rough conclusion didn't tarnish his impressive comeback in 2008. After hanging on just to get his break in the NFL, he proved his worth to the Panthers right from his very first game. And like all good quarterbacks, he'll find a way to put a bad performance behind him.

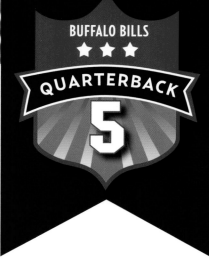

TRENT EDWARDS

BUFFALO BILLS
★ ★ ★
QUARTERBACK
5

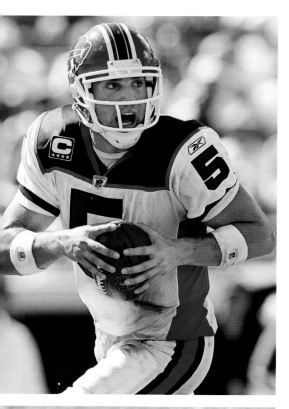

CAREER HIGHLIGHTS

- Drafted 92nd overall from Stanford University by the Buffalo Bills in 2007.
- Named to the 2007 NFL All-Rookie Team.
- Was sixth in pass completion in 2008 with a 65.5 percent completion rate.
- In 2007 won the NFL Rookie of the Week Award twice: Week 13 and 14.

Buffalo Bills quarterback Trent Edwards has always been close to his family, a way of living that began as a youngster in his hometown of Los Gatos in northern California. His two sisters, Shelby and Megan, were athletic types and Edwards would always tag along to their games. When he was about eight years old, he was tossing a football around while attending one of Shelby's volleyball games. The local high school football coach spotted the youngster tossing the ball and inquired as to who he was. When Edwards reached high school age he really had little interest in football, preferring basketball and volleyball instead. His mother, a school teacher, worried Edwards might get hurt and his father did not enjoy the one year he had played high school ball, so he was not being pushed to the gridiron. A coach convinced Edwards to come out and play quarterback for the first- and second-year high school players and eventually he became the starter of the varsity team. His pass completion mark of 78.1 percent was a national record and the team record over his last two years was 26–0.

Naturally, such a performance got him noticed by many schools and he was inundated with recruitment letters. Edwards carefully weighed all his options and decided to attend nearby Stanford University. Edwards played well at Stanford, but he had his share of injuries and bad seasons. The intelligent quarterback graduated with a degree in political science and then awaited his fate during the NFL draft. A total of five pivots were drafted ahead of him, but the Buffalo Bills called his name with the 92nd overall pick in the 2007 draft. Shelby had told her brother she would go with him no matter who selected him and he joked about the cold and snow of Buffalo should the Bills choose him. When Bills coach Dick Jauron called, Edwards was ecstatic to be drafted and Shelby still kept up her end of the bargain. The idea of moving with her brother to his new city actually came to Shelby when she heard that Tom Brady's sister had done the same thing after Brady was selected by the New England Patriots. Shelby looks after Trent's needs at his suburban Buffalo home and even a few of Edwards' teammates have come to appreciate the home cooking.

The Bills have been looking for a quarterback to lead their team since Hall of Fame member Jim Kelly left in 1996. Many believed J.P. Losman was going to fill that role, but he soon showed he was not a starting NFL passer. As a

result, Edwards played 10 games in his first season of 2007 (starting nine of them) and threw for seven touchdowns, but also gave up eight interceptions. Not many rookie quarterbacks get to start so many games, but the 6-foot-4, 231-pound Edwards showed a cool command in the pocket that the Bills immediately liked. A wrist injury to Edwards forced the Bills to go back to Losman, but only for a brief time as Buffalo finished with a 7–9 record despite an incredible amount of injuries to defensive players. By the start of the 2008 season Edwards was declared the starting QB for a Buffalo squad thought to be on the rise.

Buffalo lived up to the expectations early by going 3–0 and then winning five of their first six games. Edwards was showing a propensity for late-game heroics, securing four Buffalo comebacks in the fourth quarter. He completed 65.5 percent of his passes with 11 touchdowns, but was sacked 23 times and gave up 10 interceptions.

IN THE HUDDLE
Edwards was ranked the No. 2 pro-style quarterback coming out of high school in 2001.

Unfortunately, injuries were once again a problem for Edwards. He missed two games with a groin injury and he also suffered a concussion against Arizona in the fourth week of the season. Eventually the team fell back to a 7–9 record.

The Bills are one of the better running teams in the league and need Edwards to develop the passing game to the point where they can control the ball more. The Bills may have to consider rolling Edwards out from the pocket more often to emphasize a shorter passing game, which is more suitable for the still-developing young pivot. The hope is that the addition of colorful wide receiver Terrell Owens will give Edwards another capable target; the danger is that he could also have a negative effect on the young QB. Not that Edwards is concerned, he championed the signing of Owens right from the start.

JOE FLACCO

BALTIMORE RAVENS
★ ★ ★
QUARTERBACK
5

His NFL baptism immediately had fans in Baltimore believing the rookie quarterback was no ordinary Joe. The fact gangly Joe Flacco was the starter when the Ravens kicked off 2008 against the Cincinnati Bengals had a "pre-ordained" tinge to it.

The Ravens figured Flacco would eventually be their No. 1 man, but then destiny entered the picture and the idea of a gradual entry into the role fell by the wayside.

Joseph Vincent Flacco, born in Audubon, New Jersey, on January 16, 1985, was the second quarterback selected in the 2008 NFL draft.

IN THE HUDDLE
Flacco is the only rookie QB in NFL history to win two playoff games.

The Ravens liked his smarts, felt his play in a cold-weather place like small-school Delaware would be useful and couldn't help but be taken by an arm that was both rocket-like and accurate. Seniors Flacco and Matt Ryan of Boston College emerged as the best QBs following the NFL scouting combine and heading into the 2008 draft. Ryan went No. 3 overall to the Atlanta Falcons, leaving the Ravens to swoop in and take Flacco 15 spots later at No. 18.

Troy Smith and Kyle Boller were tabbed to battle for the starting job with Baltimore in 2008. However, Boller injured a shoulder and Smith came down with tonsillitis late in the pre-season, sending the Ravens against the Bengals on Sunday, September 7, with Flacco as their starter. By the end of the afternoon, the almost 71,000 fans on hand were chanting, "Let's Go

Flacco!" He'd won them over in a season where that 17–10 opening victory was only the beginning; he went on to start every regular season game for Baltimore and three additional playoff contests to boot.

While Flacco completed 15 of 29 passes that afternoon, his third-quarter, 38-yard bootleg run for a touchdown put Baltimore ahead 17–3. It was the longest run ever by a Ravens quarterback. With each week, Flacco gained poise and confidence, truly showing his mettle after the 2–0 Ravens dropped three in a row, the last of which was a 31–3 drubbing by the Indianapolis Colts. But taking charge like a veteran, Flacco then spearheaded a four-game winning streak and 9–2 run over the final 11 games. He was the NFL's offensive rookie of the month for November, completing 83 of 140 passes for 1,060 yards, nine touchdowns and two interceptions as the Ravens won four of five games.

By season's end, he'd completed 257 of 428 passes for 2,971 yards with 14 touchdown passes and 12 interceptions. He gained 180 yards rushing on 52 attempts with two touchdowns. And, believe it or not, he caught one pass for a 43-yard gain,

putting his receiving average in a tie with teammate wide receiver Yamon Figurs (who also had one reception) for the highest yards averaged per catch in 2008.

Until the Steelers throttled the Ravens in the 2008 AFC championship (23–14), Flacco's delirious run claimed the Miami Dolphins (27–9) and the Tennessee Titans (13–10) as post-season casualties. With the win over Miami, Flacco became the third NFL rookie QB to win in his playoff debut, but first to accomplish it on the road. Flacco pulled off another first for NFL rookie quarterbacks when he won his first two playoff games.

Bill Cowher, the longtime great NFL head coach, likens Flacco to Ben Roethlisberger. Both QBs are big (Roethlisberger 6-foot-5, 241 pounds; Flacco 6-foot-6, 230 pounds);

came from smaller schools (Roethlisberger from Miami of Ohio, Flacco from Delaware); possess strong arms; can run if need be; offer solid leadership and put up similar stats in 2008 — Flacco posted 14 TDs, 12 interceptions, a 60.0 percent completion average and an 80.3 QB rating; Roethlisberger put up 17 TDs, 15 interceptions, a 59.9 percent completion average and an 80.1 QB rating. Roethlisberger's passing yardage in 2008 (3,301) ranked 14th in the NFL, while Flacco was 20th at 2,971.

Flacco thrived in football, basketball and baseball before heading to Pittsburgh for college. After redshirting in his first year, he was a backup in his second season. Seeking to play regularly he transferred to Delaware, but in the process sat out 2005. He got his wish

CAREER HIGHLIGHTS

- Flacco's 18th overall draft selection out of the University of Delaware made him the highest pick ever selected from the school.

- Earned All-American honours as a senior in 2007.

- Two-time NFL rookie of the week (Week 8 and 17).

as the No. 1 QB over 26 games at Delaware in 2006 and 2007, setting 20 school records.

The NFL rookie sensation gained popularity outside Baltimore as well. While Ryan captured the offensive rookie of the year award in 2008, online at NFL.com, Flacco was the choice of the fans for the Diet Pepsi rookie of the year. That says something about an incredible season by a talented young athlete.

NEW YORK GIANTS
★ ★ ★
QUARTERBACK
10

ELI MANNING

"The Great Escape — Super Bowl XLII." Starring Eli Manning with special guest David Tyree, Cameo appearances by Archie, Olivia, Peyton and Cooper Manning. And introducing Abby McGrew, Eli's college sweetheart and future wife.

Sounds intriguing and gripping with action, doesn't it? Guaranteed to captivate and entertain. At the same time, it's a testimony to the emergence of New York Giants quarterback Eli Manning, who carved out his own larger-than-life image within the iconic Manning clan.

It was on February 3, 2008 in Glendale, Arizona, that Manning pulled off the Harry Houdini getaway against the 18–0 New England Patriots. The march began at the Giants 17-yard line with 2:39 to play and New England back in front courtesy of a Tom Brady-to-Randy Moss six-yard pass three seconds earlier.

The Giants converted one short-yardage fourth-down gamble and two third-down situations to snatch the victory. Running back Brandon Jacobs ran for two yards on the crucial fourth-down play to keep the yardsticks moving. Not too many remember that.

What they do recall is what occurred on the ensuing sequence with the Giants facing a third-and-five at their own 44. In the mayhem, Manning faced a massive rush with 285-pound defensive end Jarvis Green even getting a hand on him. Instead of collapsing, Manning shook free and put the ball in the air. Somehow, some way, David Tyree caught the ball on the side of his helmet and held on despite the heat from safety Rodney Harrison. Gain of 32 yards, ball on the New England 24, 59 seconds to go.

A one-yard loss when Manning was sacked and a pass incompletion had the Patriots looking good. But on third down and 11, Manning found wideout Steve Smith for 12 yards. Next play, touchdown — Manning to Plaxico Burress for 13 yards.

CAREER HIGHLIGHTS

- In 2008 was selected to his first Pro Bowl.
- Super Bowl XLII Most Valuable Player.
- Eli Manning is the seventh No. 1 pick in the NFL Draft to start a Super Bowl at quarterback.
- Was named the 2004 Cotton Bowl MVP when he lead the University of Mississippi over Oklahoma State 31–28 in his final collegiate game.

Thirty-five seconds on the clock. New York leads 17–14. The Giants defense held Brady and company, and it was game over on the Pats' bid for a perfect season.

In earning the victory, Manning had escaped more than the arms of Green. He had finally fulfilled the mighty demands of life in the Big Apple. Drafted No. 1 overall by the San Diego Chargers in 2004, Manning said he had no intention of playing for them before the draft. After the Chargers chose him, they flipped Manning to the Giants in exchange for the No. 4 pick, Philip Rivers, a third round pick in 2004 and first and fifth round selections in 2005.

IN THE HUDDLE
Eli and Peyton Manning are the only brother combination to play at quarterback in the Super Bowl and the only set of brothers to win Super Bowl MVP.

Manning had starred with the Ole Miss Rebels, his father Archie's alma mater. Born on January 3, 1981 in New Orleans, Eli was tutored at Ole Miss by David Cutcliffe, who had coached and run the same offense with Eli's brother, Peyton, during his tenure with the Tennessee Volunteers.

Manning's entry into the Giants hotbed began poorly with losses in his first six starts before his initial win in the 2004 season finale against Dallas. The following season, all that was gained by posting a record of 11–5 in the regular season dissipated with the 23–0 loss in the postseason to Carolina. In 2006, the Giants won six of their first eight games, but barely qualified for the playoffs with a record of 8–8. A quick exit followed, however, as the Philadelphia Eagles beat them 23–20.

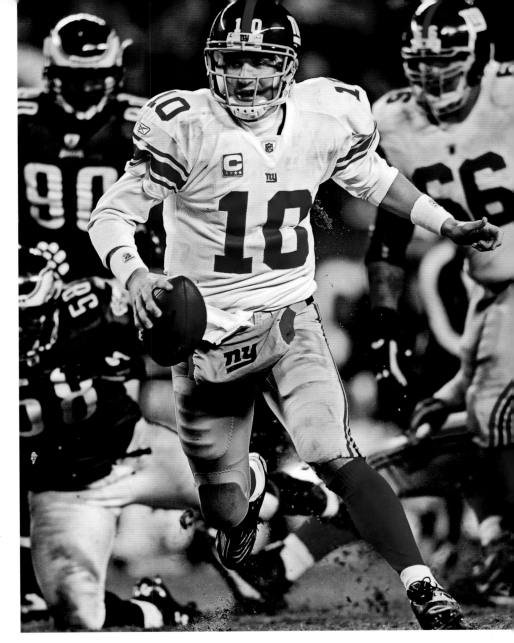

Heading into 2007, former New York running back Tiki Barber, fresh in retirement, raised questions about Manning's leadership skills. When the Giants started 2007 with back-to-back losses, the natives were restless. But they reeled off six consecutive wins and 10 in their last 14 games. In the post-season — all on the road — they upstaged Tampa Bay, Dallas and Green Bay before depriving the Pats of their unbeaten season.

Through the four playoff games, Manning completed 60.5 percent of his passes and threw six TDs with only one interception. Like Peyton in Super Bowl XLI, Eli was MVP of the NFL's championship match.

In 2008 the Giants compiled their best regular season record with Manning at 12–4 and were the NFC's No. 1 seed. He surpassed 3,200 yards passing and 21-or-more TD passes for the fourth year in a row. Yet a Super Bowl repeat was spoiled by the Eagles, who came to New York and defeated the Giants 23–11 in the divisional playoff.

There was one more game for Manning to play, though. He was off to Honolulu as a first-time Pro Bowler. He and Peyton became the first brothers to play in the same Pro Bowl game, adding another chapter to the Manning family legacy.

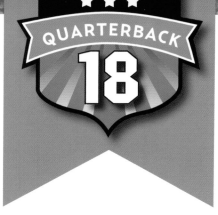

PEYTON MANNING

INDIANAPOLIS COLTS
★ ★ ★
QUARTERBACK
18

The court of popular opinion is frequently far too harsh in assessing what distinguishes a great one from being among the greatest. Fair or not, quarterback Peyton Manning endured such scrutiny, even though he'd already been a two-time NFL MVP and multi-decorated All-Pro and Pro Bowl selection when he headed into Super Bowl XLI — his first appearance in the NFL championship game since breaking into the league in 1998.

On February 4, 2007 in soggy Miami, Manning led his Indianapolis Colts to the NFL's Promised Land. That missing piece

to his checkered career arrived with the 29–17 win over the Chicago Bears. The favorable result for Manning didn't come without some adversity. Devin Hester put the Bears on the board by returning the game's opening kickoff 92 yards for a touchdown.

Manning's first series ended when his deep pass for Marvin Harrison was intercepted. But after the Colts held, Manning's next series produced his only TD pass of the game, a 53-yard strike down the middle to Reggie Wayne. When the night was over, Manning had completed 25 of 38 passes for 247 yards to earn the game's MVP.

In the aftermath of the triumph, Manning insisted the team victory was what mattered most to him, not his individual acclaim. Tony Dungy, the first black head coach to win the Super Bowl, noted Manning didn't need the NFL title to prove his Hall of Fame worthiness.

Archie and Olivia Manning raised three boys. Peyton was born in New Orleans on March 24, 1976 — two years after brother Cooper and five years before another brother, Eli. Archie was a QB of renown at Ole Miss and then with the New Orleans Saints, but he never pushed his boys into football. The fact they all took to the sport seems totally natural.

Cooper was the receiver; Peyton the quarterback and, for a time in their childhood games, young Eli was the center until going the way of the pass-thrower like his father and Peyton. At Isidore Newman High School in New Orleans, Peyton throwing passes to Cooper meant success. While a back problem curtailed Cooper's football aspirations, Peyton's climb to the NFL took him to the University of Tennessee, where he registered 33 school records, eight SEC marks and two NCAA standards.

He was the first player selected in the 1998 NFL draft as the Colts, 3–13 in 1997, banked on rebuilding around him. Indy repeated at 3–13 in Manning's rookie season, but signs he was the real deal were there with 3,739 yards passing and 26 TDs, albeit with a still career-high 28 interceptions.

IN THE HUDDLE
Manning holds four NFL rookie records for passing including, most passing attempts (575), most completions (326), most passing yards (3,739) and most touchdown passes (26).

The Colts stampeded to 13–3 in 1999, but Manning lost his first playoff game, 19–16 to the Tennessee Titans. He also suffered defeats in his second and third post-season games. The playoffs in 2003 saw him throw five TD passes in the 41–10 win at

Denver and three more in the 38–31 triumph at Kansas City. The Patriots dashed the Super Bowl dream for the Colts, however, with the 24–14 win at New England.

After a playoff win in 2004 over Denver (49–24), the high-powered Indianapolis offense was stymied and throttled by the Patriots (20–3). Manning's post-season record fell to 3–6 in 2005 when the Pittsburgh Steelers upset the Colts 21–18.

But in 2006, the Colts put it all together. They toppled Kansas City 23–8 and the Ravens 15–6 in Baltimore, but then came the Patriots threat once more. With the game in Indianapolis, it was Manning's time to shine. He keyed a stirring second-half comeback for a 38–34 AFC championship win. Since then, the

Colts have continued to be one of the NFL's marquee, high-scoring squads, but there's a new nemesis for them — the San Diego Chargers knocked them out of the playoffs in 2007 and 2008.

At 6-foot-5 and 230 pounds, Peyton has been extremely durable. Through 2008, he'd started 16 regular season games for an 11th consecutive season. He also started the 15 post-season games the Colts had played over that time. Through 2008, Manning was a seven-time All-Pro selection, nine-time Pro Bowl participant and in 2008 he added his third MVP honor to tie Brett Favre for the most all-time.

And, oh yes, he's a Super Bowl champion who's looking to augment that total.

CAREER HIGHLIGHTS
- Nine-time Pro Bowl selection (1999–2000, 2002–2008)
- His three NFL MVP awards tie him with Brett Favre for the most in league history.
- Second all time in career passing rating (94.37).
- Finished second in the 1997 Heisman voting in his senior season at the University of Tennessee.

DONOVAN McNABB

to send his veteran a strong message. Reid sent quarterback coach Pat Shurmur to tell the QB and team leader he was not playing in the second half. The Ravens went on to win 36–7, the Eagles' record dropped to 5–5–1 in the 2008 season and their playoff hopes were virtually extinguished.

IN THE HUDDLE

McNabb holds the NFL record for most consecutive passes completed over a two-game span with 24 completions.

McNabb could have sulked and ripped his coach, but playing in Philadelphia for so long has toughened his hide to the point where he can take just about anything.

Ever since he was drafted second overall by the Eagles in 1999, the 6-foot-2, 240-pound McNabb has had to prove himself to Philadelphia fans over and over again. This despite the fact he took the Eagles to the Super Bowl in 2005 — although they lost to the New England Patriots — and that he had taken Philadelphia to the NFC championship game four straight seasons between 2002 and 2005.

Throughout his time as an Eagle, McNabb adhered to the advise of those close to him — like his parents — as they urged the

quarterback to be professional and most of all to keep faith in his own abilities.

It was not always easy to do, especially when he had to deal with a teammate like wide receiver Terrell Owens, who seemed to love embarrassing the Philadelphia play-caller. Somehow, McNabb survived and ultimately thrived.

The same thing happened to close out the 2008 campaign, as the Eagles won four of their last five games to earn a playoff spot with a 9–6–1 record. The entire Philadelphia team rallied around its leader after the benching and every player seemed to realize they might be the next to sit down if Reid was willing to do this to a player of McNabb's stature. By the time the season was over, McNabb threw for a career-best 3,916 yards, and his 23 touchdowns was the third-highest regular season total in his 10-year tenure. He also had two TD completions in a 44–6 demolition of the Dallas Cowboys on the last day of the season to secure the final NFC playoff spot.

McNabb's 2008 numbers are pretty remarkable considering he didn't have a star receiver to throw to. Although Owens' personality didn't jive with McNabb's, he was still a top-notch player whom McNabb could rely on to make big plays.

Philadelphia coach Andy Reid decided he had to do something drastic. Having already watched his team tie the pitiful Cincinnati Bengals, Reid was pacing the sidelines as his club was being beaten by the defensively sound Baltimore Ravens. After 10 years of watching quarterback Donovan McNabb lead the offense, Reid decided it was time

Philadelphia's receiving corps is now more of a committee effort and includes the likes of DeShane Jackson, Reggie Brown, Kevin Curtis, Jason Avant, Brent Celek and the all-purpose running back Brian Westbrook. With the possible exception of Westbrook, none of the above can be considered go-to-guys and none — though Jackson is getting close — can be called stars. Given the circumstances, McNabb spread the ball around and had opposing defenses guessing as to where he would throw the ball. For the last stretch of season and two playoff games, it all worked perfectly.

A 26–14 win on the road over the Minnesota Vikings got the Eagles a divisional playoff date with the New York Giants in the Meadowlands and many expected Philadelphia to get steam rolled by the defending champions. But McNabb was not going to be denied

by his division rival and engineered a 68-yard drive with 1:24 to go in the first half to give the Eagles a 10–8 lead at halftime. Getting ahead seemed to give Philadelphia the lift it needed to come out in the second half and essentially shut down the Giants, ultimately walking away with a 23–11 victory.

The win over New York got McNabb and Reid back to the NFC title game together for the fifth time in their careers. Only five other quarterback-coach combinations have achieved the same level of success in league history. A slow start in Arizona hurt the Eagles badly, but they had a 25–24 lead late in the contest thanks to three TD passes by McNabb. However, the defense could not hold the Cardinals and Philly lost a chance at the Super Bowl by losing the contest 32–25. For McNabb, there was still the personal victory of proving he still belongs among the NFL's elite QBs.

CAREER HIGHLIGHTS

- Drafted second overall from Syracuse University by the Philadelphia Eagles in 1999.

- Became the third African American quarterback to start in a Super Bowl, behind Doug Williams and Steve McNair, when he did so in Super Bowl XXXIX.

- As a freshman at Syracuse, completed the longest touchdown in school history, a 96-yard throw to Marvin Harrison against West Virginia University.

- First Eagles rookie quarterback to win his first start since Mike Boryla did it in 1974 against Green Bay.

CHAD PENNINGTON

The New York Jets did not know it at the time, but their acquisition of quarterback Brett Favre from the Green Bay Packers would turn out to be one of the best things that could happen for the Miami Dolphins.

After going 1–15 in 2007, the Dolphins were looking for a quality leader to help them out of their terrible plight. The popular Pennington was released from the Jets just hours after Favre signed with the New York club, and the 32-year old pivot — who had been drafted 18th overall in the first round by the Jets in 2000 — was out $4.8 million dollars. The Dolphins stepped up

and signed Pennington to an $11.5 million, two-year deal and handed him the starting position.

Of course it helped that Bill Parcells was now in charge of the Dolphins, given that he was the one who drafted Pennington back when he was running the Jets. Parcells knew Pennington was one of the brightest quarterbacks in the NFL and possessed excellent on-field leadership. Knowing management and the coaching staff had great faith in him, Pennington went about the business of bringing Miami back into contention.

Pennington first came to

prominence while attending Marshall University, a Division II school. He and receiver Randy Moss formed quite a combination by connecting for 24 touchdowns, setting a QB-to-receiver NCAA record in the process. In 1999, his senior year, Pennington took his team to a perfect 13-0 record. His college performance got him noticed by the Jets, but he played back up for two years and did not start for New York until the 2002 season. Pennington posted a 68.9 percent pass-completion mark and threw for 22 majors with only six interceptions that year. He led the Jets to the playoffs three times during his time there (2002, 2004, 2006), but was only able to win two games in total over those seasons. He won comeback player of the year in 2006 by throwing for 3,352 yards and 17 touchdowns after sustaining two rotator cuff injuries in 2005. He was injured for most of 2007, playing only nine games in what turned out to be his final year in the Big Apple. He left the Jets holding many team records, and Pennington also held the best all-time mark in NFL history for completion percentage (65.6 percent) among all quarterbacks who had made at least 1,500 pass attempts. Perhaps it was his overall mark of 32-29 as a starter, or the fact his arm strength was always in question, that made

the Jets think they could improve on Pennington. They were proven wrong.

Miami was looking for a leader as much as anything when they gave Pennington the ball. Well prepared for any opponent, Pennington was a cool customer in the heat of battle and his teammates fed off of that for the entire 2008 season. Miami coach Tony Sparano felt Pennington was like another coach for the team, and that he could get his message out to players through his quarterback. The Dolphins posted a remarkable 11–5 record under Pennington's guidance and made their first playoff appearance since 2001. Pennington played in all 16 games and threw for 19 touchdowns while giving up just seven interceptions. The veteran pivot completed 67.4 percent of his passes and threw for a career-best single-season total of 3,653 yards. His great season also included a 24–17 victory over the Jets right in

the Meadowlands on the last day of the regular season to secure the AFC East title for Miami.

Not one to gloat or be boastful, Pennington gave all the credit for his great season to the organization and his teammates. He stated he had no interest in revenge, but was driven by the fact his work ethic and style would put him in good stead again. That was certainly the case as he was once again selected comeback player of the year, a very deserving recognition.

IN THE HUDDLE

Is the only player in NFL history to win the NFL Comeback Player of the Year Award twice: 2006 and 2008.

The only down note to the 2008 season was an AFC wild card playoff loss to the Baltimore Ravens. The Dolphins had home-field advantage, but lost the contest

CAREER HIGHLIGHTS

- Drafted 18th overall from Marshall University by the New York Jets in 2000.
- In 2008, was second in the league with a 97.4 passer rating.
- Is sixth amongst active quarterbacks with a 90.6 passer rating (eighth all time).
- Was fifth in the 1999 Heisman voting with 247 points.

27-9 with Pennington throwing an uncharacteristic four interceptions. He did complete 25 of 38 throws for 252 yards, but Miami's fate was sealed. The post-season loss keeps Pennington's playoff record as the only blemish on what has been a fine career. Surrounded by a bevy of young players, Pennington may yet be able to get his team to a Super Bowl.

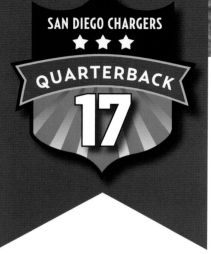

PHILIP RIVERS

San Diego Chargers quarterback Philip Rivers is a pretty ornery player and he has a way of getting under opponents' skin with his rather loud and emotional nature. Other quarterbacks pride themselves on being super cool and under control, but Rivers believes there is nothing wrong with his competitive nature spilling over.

If he gets in the face of some people — including teammates — well, he is not worried about that because he thinks sports is about having a good time and showing you care. He does not think athletes should have to tone it down. Opponents have taken to calling the vociferous Rivers obnoxious, but even those who dislike him the most would have to admit this quarterback is a winner.

Rivers had a stellar college football career after attending North Carolina State, but the scouts seemed split about his future in the NFL. Some believed he would be a good passer, while others wondered if his college numbers were on the high side because of the lesser competition he faced. It was projected the 6-foot-5, 228-pounder would go late in the first round or maybe in the second round of the 2004 draft. But the Chargers saw something in the young pivot that defied those projections. San Diego had just completed a 4–12 season and were determined to get a "franchise quarterback" with the first pick overall. They wanted Eli Manning to be that quarterback, but he had no interest in going out to San Diego, so a deal was struck with the New York Giants. The Chargers selected Manning and the Giants took Rivers fourth overall. New York then sent Rivers with first and fifth round picks in 2005 to San Diego for Manning and a third round draft choice in 2004. It took a while for Rivers to sign with San Diego and even longer to become a starter since quarterback Drew Brees was firmly at the helm. As a result, Rivers saw very little game action over his two NFL seasons, throwing only 30 passes. However, when Brees left as a free agent in 2006, Rivers was given the starter's role.

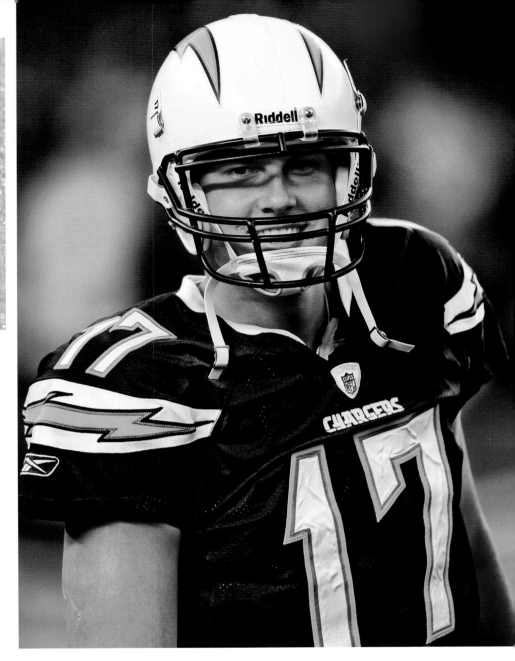

Things have not always been smooth for Rivers and the Chargers, but ever since he took over, San Diego has not missed the playoffs. The Chargers went 14–2 in 2006 as Rivers tossed 22 touchdowns and threw for 3,338 yards. Of course, it helped Rivers greatly that running back LaDainian Tomlinson had one the best years of his career, while tight end Antonio Gates and wide receiver Keenan McCardell also enjoyed great campaigns. A close 24–21 loss to New England on home field in the playoffs ended the Chargers' hopes for a Super Bowl appearance, but Rivers proved he was able to lead his team.

IN THE HUDDLE
Rivers was drafted by the New York Giants and then traded to San Diego on draft day as a part of the Eli Manning deal.

In 2007, the Chargers won their division once again with an 11–5 record and then won two playoff games before losing the AFC championship game 21–12 to the Patriots. That run gave San Diego fans hope the team was soon headed for a Super Bowl appearance.

The 2008 campaign did not go nearly so well for the Chargers and only a late-season surge in a weak division got the team into the playoffs with a mediocre 8–8 record. At one point, when the team was 4–8, there was all sorts of speculation head coach Norv Turner was going to be dismissed and there was plenty of criticism of Rivers' play. Both survived, however, and a win on the last night of the season over Denver gave San Diego the division title. The win over the Broncos seemed to be a personal vindication for Rivers, who was openly feuding with Denver quarterback Jay Cutler. Rivers finished the year with 34 touchdown passes, breaking the team record held by Dan Fouts. He also set a career mark with a total of 4,009 yards passing. The Chargers won an exciting playoff contest against the Colts and Peyton Manning, but were not really a match for the eventual Super Bowl-champion Pittsburgh Steelers, losing 35-24 one week later.

Rivers is a quarterback who is able to locate his receivers easily and gets the ball off like a rocket. He is smart and tough with ample leadership abilities — that's why Turner has always staunchly supported his QB. With the right roster moves and Rivers at the helm, San Diego may yet get that elusive Super Bowl shot.

AARON RODGERS

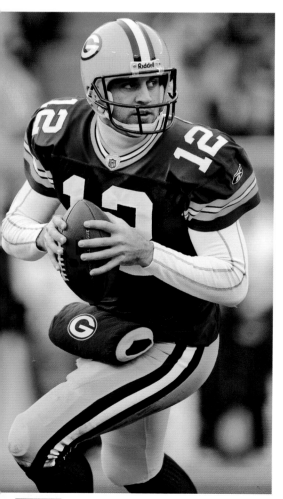

How do you try replacing a legend? The answer, quite simply, is you don't. That was the approach for quarterback Aaron Rodgers with the Green Bay Packers after Brett Favre "retired" once the 2007 season ended with an overtime loss to the New York Giants in the NFC championship.

The Packers were prepared for Favre's departure and immediately announced Rodgers would take over the offense after three seasons of minimal activity in the backup role. He'd played in seven games over that stretch, completing 35 of 59 attempts for 329 yards with one TD pass and one interception.

But at least he was schooled the Packers way, knew the offensive system and worked with Favre. The Packers were ready to move on with Rodgers and held to that commitment even after Favre declared he wanted to play another season. The Packers parted ways with Favre by shipping him to the New York Jets.

There will continue to be a lot of No. 4 jerseys in honor of Favre among Packers fans at Lambeau Field. The future Hall of Famer started every Packers game from September 27, 1992 through January 20, 2008. Rodgers knew full well he was replacing a legend and needed a little *Star Wars* love from those Favre disciples along the lines of, "May the fours be with you."

In Rodgers' first season, the Packers finished 6–10 largely because they surrendered 89 more points (380 as opposed to 291) than in their 13–3 season of 2007. The Rodgers-led offense put up 419 points to rank fifth in the NFL, almost identical to '07 when they generated 435 points to stand fourth.

The head-to-head comparison in 2008 between the 25-year-old Rodgers and the 39-year-old Favre also put the new starter in a positive light. Rodgers connected on 341 of 536 pass attempts for a completion percentage of 63.6 and 4,038 yards. He tossed 28 TDs and 13 interceptions. Favre was 343 of 522 for a 65.7 completion percentage, threw for 3,472 yards, 22 TD passes and was also picked off 22 times. Rushing wise, Rodgers carried 56 times for 207 yards and four touchdowns; Favre ran 21 times for 43 yards and one TD. Rodgers ranked fourth in 2008 in passing yards and fourth in TD passes, while Favre was 11th and ninth respectively. Favre led the league in interceptions, while Rodgers tied for the eighth-most. Following his season with the Jets, Favre once again announced his retirement and Green Bay will be stronger now that Rodgers has a year of experience under his belt.

IN THE HUDDLE

Rodgers set a University of California Golden Bears single-season record with five 300-yard passing games.

After starting the 2008 campaign with a 4–3 record, Rodgers accepted a six-year contract extension from

the Packers. The deal runs through 2014 and is reportedly worth $65 million, $20 million of that being guaranteed. Growing up in Chico, California, Rodgers was a fan of San Francisco 49ers legend Joe Montana. That affinity also eased him in taking the baton from Favre because Rodgers witnessed the 49ers torch go from his hero, Montana, to Steve Young. In his way, Young had much to prove and overcome waiting in the wings as Montana's backup when he joined the 49ers in a trade with the Tampa Bay Buccaneers. But Young earned his place in the Football Hall of Fame just as Montana did previously.

Rodgers was born December 2, 1983 and was outstanding at Pleasant Valley High School in Chico before coming under the tutelage of head coach Jeff Tedford at the University of California after transferring from Butte College. The 6-foot-2, 220-pounder was terrific in his two years with the Golden Bears, starting 22 of 25 games and passing for 5,469 yards. The Packers made Rodgers the second quarterback selected in the 2005 NFL draft at 24th overall. The 49ers had opened that draft by choosing Utah QB Alex Smith in the No. 1 position.

A terrific golfer who washed windows during the summer of 2004 in the San Francisco Bay Area, Rodgers knows he still has much to accomplish. The Packers lost seven of their last nine games in 2008. Five of those defeats were by four points or less. Turning those close games from losses to wins is what solid quarterbacks do. You can bet there will be a run on No. 12 jerseys once Rodgers puts the Pack on his back a little more often.

CAREER HIGHLIGHTS

- Ranked fourth in passing yards (4,038) and passing touchdowns (28) in 2008, his first full season as an NFL starter.
- Compiled a streak of 157 pass attempts without an interception, third longest streak in team history.
- Was named first-team All Pac 10 in 2004.
- Signed a 6-year, $65-million contract extension at the end of the 2008 season.

TONY ROMO

DALLAS COWBOYS
★ ★ ★
QUARTERBACK
9

Being quarterback of the Dallas Cowboys does have its shining-star image. There's also a steep price associated with it in a city where, in quiet times, the Cowboys are the all the rage, all the time.

When 2008 concluded on a real downer for the Cowboys and their fans — a 44–6 drubbing in Philadelphia that dumped Dallas to 9–7 and out of the playoffs — it triggered an off-season of questions surrounding Tony Romo. Is he a leader? Is he prepared to fully embrace the total responsibility of being Cowboys QB?

Legendary Dallas QB Troy Aikman, as a guest on the radio show

of another former Cowboys great, Michael Irvin, posed those very questions. He even referred back to the lingering perception created in January, 2007 when Romo and his girlfriend, Jessica Simpson, were photographed in Cabo San Lucas, Mexico, a week before the divisional playoff loss to the New York Giants.

2009 is significant chapter in Cowboys history with the opening of the new 80,000-seat Dallas Cowboys Stadium. With it, expectations are that much higher. In order to keep everyone happy, Romo's focus should be finding ways to upgrade his late-season performances.

Romo has struggled in the final month of each campaign since becoming Dallas' No. 1 man on October 29, 2006. From that time through 2008, Romo's record in December was 5–8, including 1–3 in '08. Romo is 0–2 in the post-season and on both occasions he literally had victory in his grasp. The first crushing defeat came in the wild card game at Seattle on January 6, 2007.

With 1:19 to go, Martin Gramatica was set to kick a field goal from the nine-yard line, but Romo bobbled the snap. His mad scramble got him back to the two, but one yard short of the first down. The Seahawks won 21–20.

IN THE HUDDLE
Romo leads all active NFL quarterbacks with a 94.7 career passer rating.

A season later, the Cowboys rode to home-field advantage in the NFC with a franchise-tying mark of 13–3. In the divisional playoff against the Giants — and in the aftermath of the rendezvous with Simpson in Mexico — the Cowboys were one big play away from winning. Facing a fourth-and-11 from the Giants 23, Romo's pass to the end zone intended for Terry Glenn was picked off by R.W. McQuarters for the touchback. On the next play, Eli Manning went to his knee and

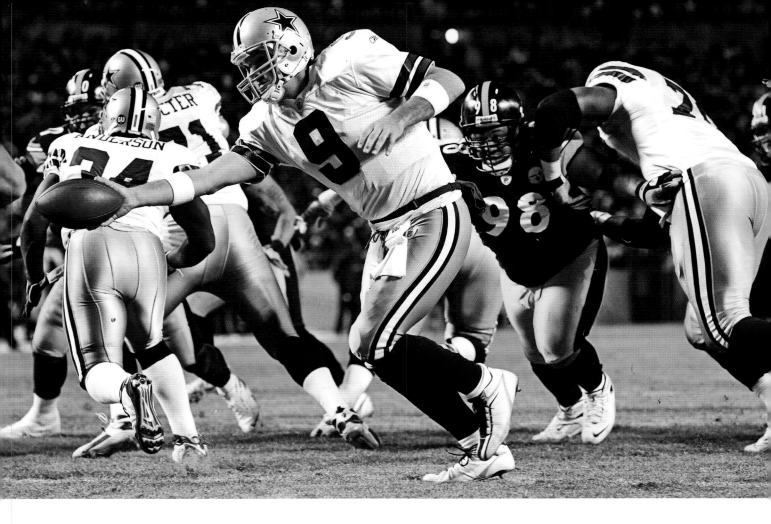

the boots were put to Dallas for that season.

On the plus side, Romo has done things in a short period of time that no other Cowboys QB can match. During 2007 in his first full season as the starter, he established club single-season records for most yards passing (4,211, the only time a Dallas QB has reached 4,000 yards in a season), completions (335), passing TDs (36) and 300-plus yard passing games (seven).

An injured baby finger in his throwing hand kept him out of three games in 2008 and the Cowboys were brutal offensively without him. When he returned, the Cowboys won three in a row and four of their next five before dropping their last two games to miss the post-season. After the season-ending loss in Philadelphia, Romo collapsed in the Cowboys locker room with a suspected rib injury, so on the physical side it was a tough year for the two-time Pro Bowler.

Antonio Ramiro Romo was born in San Diego, California, on April 21, 1980. He is the third child and only son born to Ramiro and Joan Romo. His father was serving at the large U.S. Navy base in San Diego at that time before relocating to Burlington, Wisconsin, in the summer of 1982. Romo was a natural athlete and he developed into quite a golfer while also starring in baseball, basketball, soccer and football. His football talent eventually got him to Eastern Illinois, where he left as the all-time leader in touchdown passes (85) at that school and the Ohio Valley Conference.

Undrafted in 2003, Romo signed as a rookie free agent with the Cowboys. The 6-foot-2, 224-pounder saw no NFL regular season game action in 2003, but was the reserve for six games in 2004 and 16 in 2005. He started the final 10 games of 2006 and gained the long-term endorsement of Cowboys

CAREER HIGHLIGHTS

- Named to the Pro Bowl twice: 2006 and 2007.
- Went undrafted in 2003 out of Eastern Illinois University and was signed by the Dallas Cowboys as a free agent on May 5, 2003.
- Set a Cowboys record for consecutive games with a touchdown pass with 17 straight between 2006 and 2007.
- Active NFL leader in yards per pass completion at 12.7.

owner Jerry Jones when his contract was extended in October 2007 with a six-year, $67.5 million pact ($30-million guaranteed) through 2013.

Jones did so believing the Cowboys will eventually rule the league with Romo. Those are the lofty expectations that simply come with the QB job in Dallas.

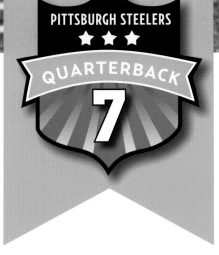

PITTSBURGH STEELERS
★ ★ ★
QUARTERBACK
7

BEN ROETHLISBERGER

The Pittsburgh Steelers usually rely on defense to secure their victories, but with 2:37 to go in Super Bowl XLIII, the Arizona Cardinals struck for a touchdown that put them up 23–20. Quarterback Ben Roethlisberger gathered the Steeler offense around him and told them all the work and preparation they had done to get to the big game was going to be for nothing if they did not drive the ball down the field and win the game.

IN THE HUDDLE
Ben, at the age of 23 years and 340 days, is the youngest starting quarterback to win a Super Bowl.

A holding penalty cost the Steelers some yards as they began their drive from their own 22-yard line. Undaunted, the cool-handed Roethlisberger hit receiver Santonio Holmes for a 14-yard gain, then on third and six, the Steeler pivot hit Holmes for a 13-yard strike. Nate Washington took another pass for 11 yards and suddenly the Steelers were at mid-field. Roethlisberger ran for four yards and then with just 1:02 to play, he connected with Holmes on a 40-yard pass-and-run play that got Pittsburgh down to the Arizona six-yard line. Two plays later, Roethlisberger spotted Holmes, this time in the back of the end zone and threw a perfect pass with three Cardinals lurking around his receiver. Holmes made an outstanding catch, dragging his toes across the end zone before falling out of bounds. Roethlisberger breathed a sigh of relief because, for a moment, he thought his pass was sure to be intercepted. The entire drive, punctuated by a TD toss that was clearly a gamble, was pure Roethlisberger in every way. The big QB's work led Pittsburgh to a 27–23 triumph.

Since joining the Steelers in 2004, all the 6-foot-5, 241-pounder has done is win. His post-season record is now 8–2 — including two Super Bowl titles — and he has won 51 regular season games in his first five years in the NFL. Roethlisberger's game is more the sum of a few parts than any one defining skill. The number of passes he completes is usually not high (66.4 percent for the 2008 season), he rarely tosses nice, tight spirals and his scrambling ability, though strong, sure isn't pretty. His running style will not remind anyone of Fran Tarkenton or Steve Young, but he loves to hold onto the ball until the last possible second. Roethlisberger is a very gritty performer and in a city that enjoys smash-mouth football, he fits in perfectly. He can play hurt and will not back down physically no matter what the circumstances. He is very capable of improvising and many of his completions look like they were drawn up on the field. His never-give-in approach has helped develop a Steeler mentality that tells every opponent, "You have to play 60 full minutes to beat Pittsburgh." Maybe that's why it so rarely happens.

Roethlisberger's linebacker approach has resulted in some trouble. Off the field, he suffered career-threatening injuries after getting into a motorcycle accident while not wearing a helmet in 2006. He has also refused to wear a newer football helmet that would aid in preventing concussions, preferring instead to keep the older model, which he is more comfortable wearing. The Steelers have not been as good a running team over the last two years and the offensive line is not as strong as it used to be, so Roethlisberger has been smacked on more than one occasion. However, the large quarterback insists the only way he'll leave the field is if he's carted off, and in the last game of the 2008 regular season against Cleveland, that's exactly what happened.

Despite all these things, Roethlisberger has matured since he entered the league after a college career at Miami of Ohio. He was a wreck before and during the first Super Bowl he played in, finishing with only nine completions on 21 attempts for a mere 123 yards, though the Steelers still beat the Seahawks 21–10. However, against the Cardinals Roethlisberger was 21 of 30 for 256 yards, starting and ending the game with two beautifully directed drives. Roethlisberger's leadership skills can no longer be questioned and his stated goal is to win more Super Bowls than legendary Steelers quarterback Terry Bradshaw, who won four Vince Lombardi Trophies. Roethlisberger now has two NFL titles under his belt and while winning five will be a tough task, there should be no underestimating this proven winner.

CAREER HIGHLIGHTS

- 2004 NFL offensive rookie of the year.
- Pro Bowl selection in 2007.
- Most wins as a starting NFL quarterback in their first five seasons (51).
- Holds the University of Miami (Ohio) Redhawks record for career total offence (11,075 yards).

MATT RYAN

The Atlanta Falcons looked like a defeated team when the Chicago Bears scored a touchdown with just 11 seconds to play to take a 20–19 lead in Week 6. The hometown fans were lingering, hoping the Falcons might pull out a miracle; not many were optimistic. But the Bears opted for a low, squiggle kickoff technique and it was returned to the Falcons 44-yard line with just six seconds left on the clock. Atlanta rookie quarterback Matt Ryan took to the field, knowing he didn't have many options for getting into field goal

range. Showing great poise under pressure, Ryan tossed a picture-perfect 26-yard pass to receiver Michael Jenkins, who managed to get out of bounds with one tick left one the clock. Kicker Jason Elam stepped up to nail a 48-yard field goal to give Atlanta a 22–20 victory. The crowd that remained went wild with celebration. The game against Chicago was a prelude to how the rest of an exciting 2008 season would go for the new-look Falcons.

Few players were as popular in Atlanta as highly talented

quarterback Michael Vick was during his time with the Falcons. But when Vick was sent to prison after his conviction for his involvement in a dog fighting ring in 2007, the Atlanta franchise was rudderless and in need of new management and players. Unknown Thomas Dimitroff was named GM in January of 2008 and he selected Mike Smith, a longtime assistant coach in the league, just a few days later to guide the team at field level. The two new leaders released many well-established players in Atlanta and

CAREER HIGHLIGHTS

- Was named the ACC's player of the year as a senior in college.

- Is only the second player in NFL history to throw for a touchdown on his first pass when he connected with Michael Jenkins in the end zone on a 62-yard pass.

- Only the second rookie in NFL history to compile 3,000 passing yards.

- Was named NFC rookie of the month in October 2008.

then made their most important decision at the 2008 NFL draft. The Falcons held the third pick of the draft by virtue of their 4–12 record in 2007 and were thinking about selecting defensive tackle Glenn Dorsey. However, Dimitroff realized he might not have the opportunity to nab a quality quarterback in the later rounds or even in the following year's draft. Ryan was seen as the most NFL-ready pivot available, so the Falcons took the 6-foot-4, 220-pound Boston College graduate. Ryan's main attributes included his ability to conquer the mental side of the game, plus his ultra-competitive nature.

Smith decided he would make the quarterback position available to whoever rightfully earned the spot. Ryan was up against Chris Redman, Joey Harrington and D.J. Shockley, and he beat them all for the starting job. He never surrendered his role for the rest

of the season, compiling an 11–5 record — second best in the NFC South to Carolina's 12–4 mark — while throwing 3,440 yards and 16 touchdowns.

IN THE HUDDLE
Ryan set a NFL playoff rookie record with 26 completions in a single post-season game.

He showed all the skills that made him such a high pick and gained him the richest rookie contract in NFL history — $72 million over six years. His teammates were very impressed with his calm demeanor and for showing a maturity that belied his 23 years. He had his rookie moments, but those times were few in number, and he produced nine games where he passed for 200 or more yards. He was also able to gain valuable playoff experience with a 30–20 wild card game loss to the surging

Arizona Cardinals, managing to throw two touchdown passes.

Assuming the Falcons can keep their lineup largely intact, Ryan will have many weapons at his disposal. Running back Michael Turner was a steal as a free agent signing, while receiver Roddy White looks like he has a great career ahead of him and the offensive line performed better than anyone had hoped at the beginning of the year. The Falcons said they were not going to measure success in 2008 by wins and losses, but many things went well, not the least of which was Ryan's performance. His campaign was capped by being named the NFL's offensive rookie of the year.

The Atlanta organization has been through a great deal over the last two seasons, but the face of the club has changed and fans will soon forget about wearing their "Vick" jerseys and start to buy team colors with No. 2 on the front and "Ryan" on the back.

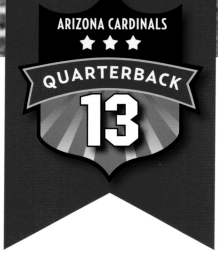

KURT WARNER

The life and times of quarterback Kurt Warner are worthy of Hollywood, reality TV and a gripping novel. He's a feel-good story; an inspiration; a family guy devoted to his wife, Brenda, and their seven kids; an individual with deep faith and a credit to all the community endeavors he and his wife lend their passionate support to.

You see him named recipient of the Walter Payton Man of the Year Award for his volunteer/ charity work and his excellence on the field *before* Super Bowl XLIII and you say, "Good for him." Then you sit back and watch his dazzling act in amazement.

Kurt Warner was born on June 22, 1971 in Burlington, Iowa. He was stocking shelves in a grocery store at $5.50 an hour *after* he was cut by the Green Bay Packers in 1994. All the while, he never gave up on his desire to make it as an NFL quarterback.

He became an Arena Football League great with the Iowa Barnstormers from 1995 to 1997, then headed to NFL Europe to play for the Amsterdam Admirals in 1998. Later that year an injury to Trent Green got him some NFL regular season game action with the St. Louis Rams. Then, he unleashed an offensive explosion never seen before as the on-field leader of "The Greatest

Show on Turf." The Warner-led Rams scored an unprecedented 500-plus points a season for three seasons in a row: from 1999 through 2001.

Warner was a two-time NFL MVP (in 1999 and 2001), Super Bowl XXXIV MVP and sitting on top of the world. Or so it seemed. By 2003, he was out of his starter's job with the Rams in favor of Marc Bulger. Off to New York, Warner was custodian of the No. 1 spot with the Giants long enough to get incoming Eli Manning prepped to take over.

Then Warner headed to Arizona in 2005 and many asked if he was that pro who just didn't know when to quit. First, he and

CAREER HIGHLIGHTS

- Super Bowl XXXIV MVP.
- Four-time Pro Bowl selection (1999–2001, 2008).
- Tied with Steve Young and Rich Gannon as the only quarterbacks to have six consecutive games with 300 or more passing yards.
- Has the second-highest career pass completion percentage in NFL history at 65.4 percent.

Josh McCown jockeyed for the starting position. Then, it would become Matt Leinart as perhaps the long-term fix for the Cards. Somehow, Warner just kept doing what he's always done, never taking himself out of the picture and then turning back the time machine for a return to glory.

IN THE HUDDLE
Kurt Warner holds the NFL record for passing yards per game at 259.1 ypg.

In 2008, using Larry Fitzgerald and Anquan Boldin as his favorite targets, Warner transformed the moribund franchise into a Super Bowl contender. He guided the No. 2 offense in the NFL in passing yards per game (292.1) and No. 4 in per-game total offense (365.8). With 427 points on the board, the Cardinals were tied for No. 3 in the league. Warner compiled 4,583 yards passing (ranked second), 30 TD passes (third in the NFL) and a passing efficiency of 96.9 (No. 3). For the fourth time in his career, Warner was a Pro Bowl selection as the Cardinals won their first-ever NFC West title and reached the playoffs for the first time since 1998.

Arizona topped Atlanta, Carolina and Philadelphia in the post-season to advance to the championship game. As far as dramatic spectacles are concerned, Super Bowl XLIII didn't disappoint. When Warner is involved in any title match, thrills are guaranteed. It happened in Super Bowl XXXIV when the Rams scored late to beat Tennessee 23–16 on a Warner-to-Isaac Bruce 73-yard score with less than two minutes to play. Of course, St. Louis

still needed a final game-saving tackle by Mike Jones on Kevin Dyson at the one-yard line on the game's final play.

In Super Bowl XXXVI, Warner-to-Ricky Proehl for 26 yards tied it 17–17 with 90 seconds to go. But New England won it when Adam Vinatieri booted a 48-yard field goal as time expired. And it happened once more when the 6-foot-2, 218-pound Warner, at 37, found a way to get the Cardinals back in front with 16 points in the fourth quarter against the

Steelers in 2009. His 64-yard connection with Fitzgerald as the clock showed 2:37 on the board had Arizona ahead 23–20. Credit the Steelers though, they needed a heart-stopping, clutch drive and they got it for the 27–23 win.

Warner's passing yardage in his three Super Bowls — 414 against Tennessee, 377 versus Pittsburgh and 365 against New England — are the three highest totals in the game's history. Selection to the Pro Football Hall of Fame is all that's required to complete Warner's football saga.

RUNNING BACKS

MARION BARBER — Dallas Cowboys

RONNIE BROWN — Miami Dolphins

MATT FORTE — Chicago Bears

FRANK GORE — San Francisco 49ers

RYAN GRANT — Green Bay Packers

STEVEN JACKSON — St. Louis Rams

BRANDON JACOBS — New York Giants

CHRIS JOHNSON — Tennessee Titans

THOMAS JONES — New York Jets

JAMAL LEWIS — Cleveland Browns

MARSHAWN LYNCH — Buffalo Bills

ADRIAN PETERSON — Minnesota Vikings

CLINTON PORTIS — Washington Redskins

STEVE SLATON — Houston Texans

LADAINIAN TOMLINSON — San Diego Chargers

MICHAEL TURNER — Atlanta Falcons

BRIAN WESTBROOK — Philadelphia Eagles

DALLAS COWBOYS
★ ★ ★
RUNNING BACK
24

MARION BARBER

For a man nicknamed "Marion the Barbarian," Dallas Cowboys running back Marion Barber is an awfully quiet person. He does his best to shun the media spotlight, rarely giving interviews. On one occasion, he did let a television show film him while he played the piano at his downtown Dallas condo. Barber is very good with his teammates, who respect him as a player and a person, and he can be very funny in the right company. But to those who aren't close to him, Barber can come across as a man with an angry scowl.

On the field Barber is all business, a bruising running back who wants to initiate contact. He will not try to find a way around a tackler. He prefers to lower his head and shoulders and run right over them, almost like he had something personal against each member of the other team. Though Barber is a hard runner, he is also deceptively fast and can get down the field in a hurry once past the line of scrimmage. He has a great ability to cut back against the grain to find an open area and with his approach to hitting, few opponents want to tackle him without some help. Built solidly at an even 6-foot and 220 pounds, Barber excels around the goal line with a great determination to score.

The Cowboys were not sure they were getting anything more than a short-yardage back when they selected Barber in the fourth round of the 2005 NFL draft with the 109th selection. But Dallas owner Jerry Jones liked what he saw — especially after the 2007 season when Barber had 975 yards rushing for a 4.8 average and 10 TDs along the ground — and let running back Julius Jones sign as a free agent with Seattle so that Barber would become

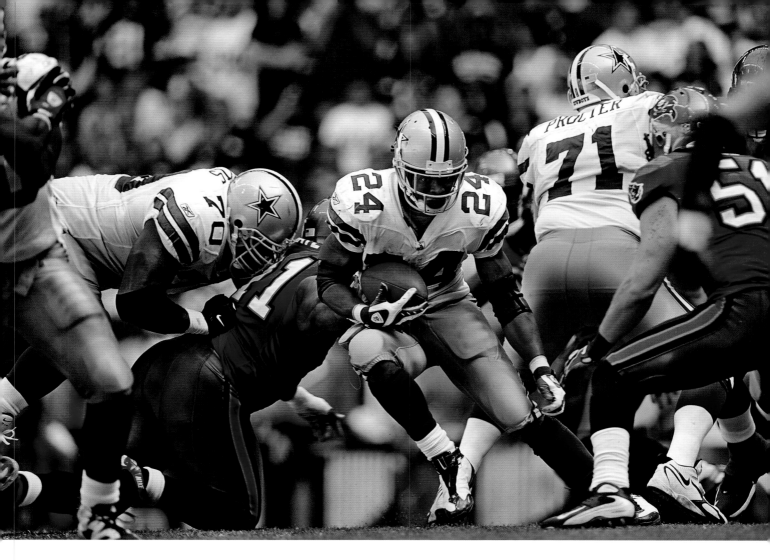

the featured back in the Cowboys offense. Dallas signed Barber to a $45-million contract, which included $16 million in guaranteed bonus payments. The first three years of his new deal put him in the company of some of the best backs in the NFL, even though he had actually started just one game in the 2007 season.

Barber likely gets his athletic prowess from his father, also named Marion, who was a running back with the New York Jets in the 1980s. The son was very good not only at football, but baseball and track and field. He played both ways in his senior year of high school and then played college football at the University of Minnesota, just like his father years earlier. He rushed for 35 all-time touchdowns (one more than his father had over his college career) and shared the backfield duties with Laurence Maroney, now a very

good player for the New England Patriots. Barber decided to skip his senior year to turn professional and the Cowboys gave him the ball 138 times as a rookie for 538 yards and a very respectable five touchdowns. Barber had roughly the same stats the next year, but scored 14 TDs along the ground in 2006.

IN THE HUDDLE

Barber scored 16 total touchdowns in 2006, tied for first in the NFC and third in the NFL.

Dallas head coach Wade Phillips was on the coaching staff of the Houston Oilers (with his father Bum) when they employed star running back Earl Campbell. Barber does not have the bulk of Campbell, but does possess his charging-bull style. Phillips likes Barber's explosive nature, but also

the fact he's elusive enough to make people miss. He also likes that Barber is an all-purpose back who can run, catch and provide great blocks for quarterback Tony Romo. To help Barber out, the Cowboys spent a first round pick on running back Felix Jones, who provides a change of pace for the attack.

The Cowboys looked like a sure thing for the playoffs in 2008, winning three of their first four games. But injuries to key players held Dallas to a 9–7 mark and no post-season action. Barber was doing very well, but an injury to his toe derailed his season, leaving him with 885 yards rushing and an average per-carry under 4.0. Barber prepares himself very well and will work to rebound and recapture his Pro Bowl status. He and Felix Jones should give Dallas a solid one-two punch out of the backfield for the next few years.

RONNIE BROWN

The Miami Dolphins were decided underdogs when they traveled to New England for their third game of the 2008 season. The Dolphins had already lost their first two contests and were coming off a 2007 campaign that saw them win just one of 16 games. Miami's roster featured 27 new players in 2008, plus a rookie head coach in Tony Sparano. The Patriots had not lost in 21 regular season games and even though they had lost Tom Brady for the season, the Dolphins still didn't seem like much of a threat.

But something magical happened that Sunday afternoon in September that changed Miami's fortunes — and running back Ronnie Brown was the man leading the way.

Miami scored first when Brown ran the ball in from two yards out to give the Dolphins a 7–0 lead in the first quarter. Before the first half was over, Brown scored two more touchdowns on runs of 15 and five yards, upping Miami's lead to 21–6. In the third quarter, Brown threw a 19-yard pass to teammate Anthony Fasano to make it 28–6. And then to finish his brilliant day, Brown ran for a 62-yard major as the Dolphins romped to a 38–13 victory. In all, Brown ran for a total of 113 yards along the ground on 17 carries, caught one pass for nine yards and completed his only pass for a major score. A big reason for Brown's success was a new formation the Dolphins instituted for the game — a direct snap to their star running back. Given a few extra yards to assess what the defense was doing, Brown was able to pick his way through the totally befuddled Patriots defense.

It was a day of redemption for Brown and the start of something not seen in the NFL since the days of the "single wing" offense. That old formation emphasized blocking to attack at a particular point, allowing tailbacks — like Brown — to pose the triple threat of running, throwing or handing off. As the season wore on Miami's updated version became known as the "wildcat offense." Soon other teams were copying the formation, but few could do it as well as the Dolphins because they did not have a versatile performer like Brown in the backfield.

IN THE HUDDLE
Brown's five touchdowns versus New England in Week 3 of 2008 set the Dolphins single-game TD record.

Brown became a Dolphin after he was selected second overall in the 2005 NFL draft following his college career at Auburn University. The Dolphins were enthralled with Brown's power and speed and the fact he could take a beating and still be productive late in games.

His rookie year in Miami saw him rush for 907 yards on 207 carries with 32 catches tacked on. In his second season, Brown recorded 1,008 yards and caught 33 passes,

and he was on his way to a career year in 2007 when a serious knee injury stopped his season after just seven games. The 6-foot, 230-pound back was facing a major rehabilitation period with a torn ACL, but he worked very hard and was ready for the Dolphins training camp in August. It was a remarkable recovery considering a reconstructed knee often takes upwards of an entire year to fully heal.

However, management's questions about Brown went well beyond his knee. A courteous and polite person, Brown is still very close to his small-town roots (Rome, Georgia) and is generally a humble sort. Seen as too easygoing and not intense enough, Brown was shuffled around somewhat and even made a kickoff return when he had no such previous experience.

The Dolphins signed free agent Ricky Williams, a 31-year old on-again off-again NFLer, to help out in the backfield, but Brown was unfazed by it all. He rushed for 916 yards in 2008, scoring 10 TDs along the ground and hauling 33 passes out of the backfield. He showed a good attitude and a willingness to embrace change, even if it meant he — and not quarterback Chad Pennington — was running a new formation at times. Brown, named as a reserve for the 2009 Pro Bowl, has made it all the way back and is once again a valued member of the Dolphins.

CAREER HIGHLIGHTS

- His four rushing touchdowns against New England in 2008 is a Dolphins record.
- His 10 rushing TDs in 2008 was the eighth highest in the NFL.
- Brown's four consecutive 100-yard rushing games rank second most in team history.
- His 207 rushing attempts in 2005 is the second best mark for a Dolphin rookie.

CHICAGO BEARS
★ ★ ★
RUNNING BACK
22

MATT FORTE

CAREER HIGHLIGHTS

- One of eight rookies since 1970 to lead his team in rushing yards and receptions.
- One of eight rookies with 1,000-plus rushing yards and 50-plus receptions in NFL history.
- Rushed for 2,127 yards as a senior at Tulane University; seventh all-time in NCAA history.

Lucas Oil Stadium, the new digs of the Indianapolis Colts, was gushing with pride to host its first-ever NFL regular season game on Sunday, September 7, 2008. The Colts hadn't lost a game in the first two months of a season since dropping one in Kansas City on October 31, 2004. Their streak since then stood at 21 games, two shy of the 23 won by the Green Bay Packers from 1928 to 1932.

So it was natural the Colts were the odds-on favorites to beat the Chicago Bears in Week 1 of 2008.

But Matt Forte, the first rookie running back to start a season with the Bears since the legendary Walter Payton in 1975, had different ideas. He racked up as impressive a first game as one could ask for: 123 yards rushing on 23 carries, including a speedy dash for his longest run of the season (a 50-yard TD) in the first quarter, plus three receptions for 18 yards. No other Bears rookie had rushed for as many yards in his first NFL game.

The kid from the Tulane Green Wave was only just beginning a season where he'd carry the ball 316 times for 1,238 yards and eight touchdowns augmented by 63

pass receptions for 477 yards and four TDs. His combined 1,715 yards from scrimmage set a record for Chicago rookies, shattering the mark of another beloved running back, Gale Sayers (1,374 in 1965).

IN THE HUDDLE
Forte was named rookie of the week in Week 12 of the 2008 NFL season.

Forte rushed for more than 100 yards in a game three times in 2008, with his season high coming at St. Louis in Week 12, where he posted 139 yards rushing and two TDs on 21 attempts. He put together 11 games of more than 100 combined yards from scrimmage, including a streak of six games in a row from Weeks 9 through 14. While no one was going to touch Atlanta QB Matt Ryan for the NFL Offensive Rookie of the Year Award in 2008, only four rookies in total earned votes and Forte was one of them.

The 6-foot-2, 216-pounder impressed his veteran teammates with his quick adjustment to the pro game along with his comfort in both the ground game and in the air. By season's end, those looking back at the 2008 NFL draft believe the

Bears lucked out in getting Forte in the second round at 44th overall. He was the sixth running back selected in that draft and first in the second round. The first round picks were Darren McFadden of Arkansas (No. 4 to the Oakland Raiders), Oregon's Jonathan Stewart (No. 13 to the Carolina Panthers), Felix Jones of Arkansas (No. 22 to the Dallas Cowboys), Rashard Mendenhall of Illinois (No. 23 to the Pittsburgh Steelers) and Chris Johnson of East Carolina (No. 24 to the Tennessee Titans).

Forte was born in Lake Charles, Louisiana, on December 10, 1985. His father, Gene, preceded him at Tulane University, where he served as captain of the Green Wave in 1977. Forte's older brother,

Bryan, was also into football at the collegiate level with McNeese State. Forte credits his father as his biggest influence, starting from the initial stages when he was his coach and then later when he had to choose post-secondary education. His father's Tulane ties weighed heavily on his decision to stay in his home state.

Forte was an excellent student while starring at Slidell High School in Slidell, Louisiana. Making the grade there academically went hand-in-hand with his standout play in football, where he was the St. Tammany Parish (county) player of the year as a senior.

Forte studied finance at Tulane, believing a degree from the respected school would always

serve well if his aspirations at an NFL career were somehow thwarted. He was a four-year letterman who left the Green Wave as the school's all-time leader in touchdowns (44), rushing touchdowns (39) and average rushing yards per game (99.186).

In Forte's last amateur game, the 2008 Senior Bowl in Mobile, Alabama, he garnered the game's MVP selection for game highs in rushing yards (58 yards on eight carries) and receptions (four for 38 yards). Although it was expected he'd have to battle for his starting spot in the Bears backfield, Forte won it from the outset. His first NFL game at Indianapolis told the world he was ready.

FRANK GORE

Running Back Frank Gore exhibits a certain type of passion virtually every time his number is called. Inside or outside, on running plays or on passing calls, he possesses the ability to break clear and find his way to the house. This bundle of excitement for the San Francisco 49ers is his own West Coast offense and there's a keen sense Candlestick Park is on the verge of being re-lit by success on the gridiron.

And burning bright in the aftermath of setbacks is something

Gore, born May 14, 1983, has confronted numerous times to arrive where he is now: an NFL star on the up, making a comfortable living to support his family just like he promised he would when the left the University of Miami a year early.

His mother, Liz, remains his inspiration and guiding light even though she succumbed to her long battle with kidney disease in September 2007. His mother had been on dialysis three times a week ever since Gore was in the 11th

Grade at Coral Gables High School. Among the leading factors for his choosing the Miami Hurricanes was to remain home and be there for her and his brother and sister.

A single mother living on welfare, Liz Gore raised her children in a one-bedroom apartment in a drug-infested area of Coconut Grove, Florida. Often the two-room apartment was over-crowded as Liz offered refuge to other family members who needed help.

She guided her son through his problems with dyslexia and ensured he steer clear of the pitfalls that had ruined so many other lives in their neighborhood. At UM, Gore twice overcame serious knee injuries, the second of which sent him into near depression.

IN THE HUDDLE
Gore led the NFC in rushing yards in 2006 with 1,695 yards.

With his battered knees, it was no surprise that the 5-foot-9, 217-pounder didn't go until the third round of the 2005 NFL draft; the 49ers selected him 65th overall. Armed with a pro contract, Gore then made two things a priority: he put his mother in a new home and he set about becoming the dynamic running back he felt he could be.

Liz lived long enough to see

her son accomplish a great deal in a short period of time. He played 14 games in his rookie NFL season with only one start, but he was still good enough to lead the 49ers in rushing with 608 yards on 127 carries. He also glimpsed a pass-catching ability with 15 receptions for 131 yards.

Gore then exploded in 2006 with an All-Pro/Pro Bowl season that put him into the 49ers record book in numerous categories. He set franchise records over a season for carries (312), rushing yards (1,695), combined rushing and pass-receiving yards (2,180) and most 100-yard rushing games in a season (nine, shattering by three the mark shared by a couple of 49er greats, Roger Craig in 1988 and Garrison Hearst in 1998). The Pro Bowler had finished first in the NFC and third in the NFL in rushing yards and he showed his breakaway burst frequently in pacing the league with

15 carries of 20-plus yards.

During that off-season, Gore and the 49ers extended their commitment to each other with a contract extension through 2011 worth about $28 million. As the months progressed, however, other issues put a damper on that euphoria. Gore sustained a broken hand during that pre-season, then dealt with the impact of losing his mother. Finally, he battled an ankle injury that lingered throughout the year. But he still rushed for 1,102 yards and paced the 49ers with 53 catches for 436 yards. He also entered exclusive company in 49ers history as the fifth player to rush for more than 1,000 yards in back-to-back seasons, joining Joe Perry (1953–54), Craig (1988–89), Hearst (1997–98) and Charlie Garner (1999–2000).

Gore broke free of that pack in 2008, even though he missed games at Miami and St. Louis in Weeks 15

CAREER HIGHLIGHTS

- Has compiled three consecutive 1,000 yard seasons from 2006–2008.
- Collected both Pro Bowl and All Pro honours in 2006.
- Set high school records in Dade County Florida when he rushed for 2,953 yards and 28 touchdowns as a senior.

and 16 because of an ankle injury. He returned for San Francisco's final game of the season and rushed 11 times for 58 yards. That total pushed his rushing production for the season to 1,036 yards, as he became the first 49er with three-consecutive 1,000-yard rushing seasons.

Over his first four seasons, Gore's stats line showed 5,866 yards: 4,441 rushing and 1,425 pass-receiving yards. This young man has shown he *can* overcome, just like his mother taught him.

RYAN GRANT

Ryan Grant's path to NFL stardom has been defined by the sharp contrasts of delight and despair, not unlike a Shakespearian protagonist trying to obtain a goal while traversing through the peaks and valleys that life has to offer.

For the Green Bay running back, sometimes those incredible lows and remarkable highs have occurred in the same game. And no one contest stands as a better example than the divisional playoff played between the Packers and the Seattle Seahawks on the snowy stage of Lambeau Field on January 12, 2008.

IN THE HUDDLE
Grant's streak of six consecutive games with a rushing TD in 2008 ties the second longest streak in Green Bay history.

It only took 20 seconds for Seattle to open the scoring of that playoff contest after Grant fumbled on the game's first play from scrimmage. The ensuing Green Bay offensive series wasn't much better either as Grant fumbled for the second time, derailing any momentum gained by a few solid Green Bay plays. The Grant miscue allowed Seattle to take a 14–0 lead just over four minutes into the game.

The embattled running back eventually came through for his team toward the end of the first quarter with a one-yard touchdown to knot the game a 14. The rest of the contest was dominated by the legendary Packer defense, which allowed a mere six points over the last three quarters. Green Bay went on to win 42–20, largely because of Grant's play: 27 rushes for 201 yards, including a 43-yard romp, and three touchdowns. His rushing yardage total broke the Packers record for rushing yards in a playoff game, surpassing Ahman Green's 156-yard performance at Philadelphia on January 11, 2004.

A week later, the Giants defense held Favre and Grant in check to knock the Packers out in the NFC championship in overtime at Lambeau. While that game marked the end of the Favre era with Green Bay, Grant would return for more.

His 956 rushing yards for the Packers in 2007 lasted briefly as a career high because Grant accumulated 1,203 yards on the ground — ninth best in the league — in 2008. He ranked sixth in the NFL with an average of 19.5 carries per game. The 6-foot-1, 226-pounder from Nyack, New York, is a powerful back who goes right at opponents and battles for every yard.

Grant graduated from Don Bosco Prep School in Ramsey, New Jersey, heading for Notre Dame with impressive high school performances in football, basketball and track. His finest season with the Fighting Irish came as a sophomore when he rushed for 1,085 yards. Grant left Notre Dame with 2,200 rushing yards and 18 touchdowns.

After an injury plagued senior year, Grant declared himself eligible for the 2005 NFL draft. He went unpicked and signed with the Giants as a non-drafted free agent and spent the season on their practice roster. The struggling running back was then in an accident that almost took his life and sidelined him for the entire 2006 season.

While at a nightclub Grant was bumped and in an attempt to stabilize himself, he crashed into Champagne glasses on the table he was near, cutting an artery, a tendon and the ulnar nerve in his left arm. He bled profusely and underwent emergency surgery. He was told by medical officials he may not regain feeling in his left hand, and during the rehab process he had to learn things as simple as how to hold a fork and spoon again.

Grant became the feel-good story of 2007. After being traded by the running back-rich Giants to Green Bay for sixth round draft pick, he had to bide his time with brief appearances until opportunity knocked in Week 8 when DeShawn Wynn sustained an injury. Once Grant got into regular action, he played like a man possessed, rushing 22 times for 104 yards. In those final 10 games of 2007, he rushed for 929 yards — a total only surpassed by LaDainian Tomlinson, who had but 18 more yards in the same 10-game span.

Grant is grateful for every day he gets to play in the NFL, and given all the adversity he has overcome to make it, the title of Shakespeare's play, *All's Well That Ends Well*, seems to fit this protagonist.

CAREER HIGHLIGHTS

- Was ninth in rushing yards in the NFL in 2008 with 1,203 yards.
- His 5.1-yard rushing average was the fifth highest in the NFL in 2007.
- Was the 13th running back in Notre Dame history to top 2,000 yards rushing in his college career.

STEVEN JACKSON

Las Vegas born and raised, Steven Jackson isn't one to play the tables or the slots. His parents, Steve and Brenda, watched a lot of people blow their money over the years and quickly stemmed any gambling instinct their son might have. After serving in Vietnam and moving to Vegas from Warren, Arkansas, in 1970, Steve Sr. became a porter and later long-time pit boss at Caesar's Palace; Brenda was a blackjack dealer for 22 years at the Hilton.

IN THE HUDDLE

In 2007 Jackson scored a 50-plus yard touchdown in three consecutive games becoming the first player to do so since Deuce McCallister in 2003.

Steven Jackson is hoping the odds swing in favor of the St. Louis Rams with Steve Spagnuolo now as head coach after his successful tenure as defensive coordinator for the New York Giants. Many believe Spagnuolo's hiring will prove beneficial for the multi-talented Jackson and restore him to the breakout level he achieved in 2006.

The dynamic dreadlocked running back was in his third NFL season in 2006 and he made it one to remember for the 8–8 Rams, who finished one win out of first place in the NFC West. Jackson rushed for a career-high 1,528 yards (fifth in the league in 2006) on 346 carries and 13 TDs while adding three more touchdowns from 90 receptions for 806 yards. His 2,334 yards from scrimmage topped the NFL and ranked fifth-best all-time. His rushing yardage in 2006 was the highest total by a Ram since Eric Dickerson compiled 1,821 yards 20 years before that. Jackson found his way to All-Pro and Pro Bowl honors and easily emerged as MVP of the Rams.

In the two ensuing seasons, Jackson was slowed by injuries, playing just 12 games in each of 2007 and 2008. But he still managed to extend his streak of 1,000-yard rushing seasons to four by ending 2007 with 1,002 yards and 2008 with 1,042. Those achievements did little to stem the tailspin of his Rams, who dropped to last place in the NFC West with records of 3–13 in 2007 and 2–14 in 2008.

Playing for pride each time, Jackson found a way to eclipse 1,000 yards rushing in 2007 and 2008 by coming through on the final day of the season. In 2007, he rushed for 55 yards on 18 carries in the Week 17 defeat at Arizona; a year later, he rushed

for 161 yards on 30 carries in the Week 17 loss in Atlanta.

The outspoken Jackson is frustrated by the losing as each of 2007 and 2008 finished with long winless streaks of four games and 10 games, respectively. However, as one of the final remaining players drafted by the Rams from 2000 through 2004, he's still young enough at age 25, and brimming with confidence in his ability, to remain a cornerstone with the Rams. He held out from training camp in 2008, then netted a new six-year contract worth just under $50 million, so he is in a position to be the long-term face of the franchise.

An excellent student who devoured books, Jackson also possessed dreams of one day playing in the NFL. He even wrote a poem about that aspiration when he was 10 years old and it can be read on his official web site. That same site also describes the solidly built 6-foot-2, 235-pounder as a package combining traits of Tony Dorsett, Earl Campbell, Barry Sanders and Marshall Faulk.

Jackson excelled in football, basketball and track at Eldorado High School in Las Vegas before attracting national attention with the Oregon State Beavers. He became the first Oregon State player with eligibility remaining to declare himself for the NFL draft and the Rams selected him in the first round, 24th overall in 2004.

Veterans Torry Holt and Isaac Bruce were instrumental in assisting Jackson through his early seasons when Faulk was still in the St. Louis backfield. Jackson rushed for 673 yards (on 134 carries) and caught 19 passes for 189 yards in his rookie season. He rushed for 1,046 yards and added 320 yards on pass receptions as a sophomore.

CAREER HIGHLIGHTS

- His 90 receptions in 2006 placed him sixth among running backs in NFL history in single-season receptions.
- Selected to the Pro Bowl in 2006.
- Fifth in NFL history in single-season yards from scrimmage with 2,334 yards in 2006.
- Four consecutive 1,000-yard rushing seasons (2005–2008).

The frustration of wanting to do more for the Rams ended with his massive performance in 2006 when he got his hands on the ball 436 times (346 rushing and 90 receiving).

During that off-season, Jackson even got the key to the city in Las Vegas, as one of its favorite sons was recognized for making his hometown proud.

BRANDON JACOBS

CAREER HIGHLIGHTS

- Tied for third in the NFL in 2008 with 15 rushing touchdowns.
- Was third in rushing yards per attempt with 5.0 yards per attempt in 2008.
- Led the Giants with nine touchdowns in 2006.
- Was named the NFC offensive player of the month for October 2007.

New York Giants running back Brandon Jacobs is a big man who enjoys playing a physical game. His linebacker build and mentality allows him to simply run over opposing tacklers who do not relish the thought of trying to subdue the big bruiser. His large 6-foot-4, 264-pound body lets Jacobs inflict punishment, but he also takes some hard hits because he is such an inviting target. His style has caused him some injuries and he may have to adjust by running a little closer to the ground, but the Giants are very happy to have such a huge weapon in their backfield.

Jacobs was born in Napoleonville, Louisiana, and grew in a single-parent household with his mother, Janice. He was a very good high school athlete who was given the treatment that sometimes comes along with being a teenage star. Jacobs was proficient at both basketball and football, and his senior year saw him rush for over 3,000 yards and record 38 touchdowns. His great year was noticed by Auburn University, but his lack of a high school diploma kept him out. Jacobs attended a small junior college in Kansas and enjoyed going to school along with playing football. Two years of outstanding play made Jacobs a highly sought after player and Auburn was now able to accept him. The Tigers were loaded at the running back position, featuring the likes of Ronnie Brown and Carnell "Cadillac" Williams, so Jacobs did not get much action. Knowing he would not be in the starting lineup in 2004, Jacobs went to Southern Illinois, a Division II school, so he would not have to sit out a year as he would had he attended another Division I college. He ran for 922 yards and 19 touchdowns. The NFL draft was up next, but Jacobs was seen more as a short-yardage player,

even though he was very fast.

The Giants took Jacobs with a pick in the fourth round and kept him on the team in quiet fashion since they had Tiki Barber as their main back. Jacobs did score seven times in 2005, but only carried the ball 39 times. The 2006 campaign saw him rush for 432 yards with nine touchdowns, but he was still not in a prime role. But in 2007, with Barber having retired, Jacobs rambled for 1,009 yards, averaging 5.0 per carry and he also made 23 catches. Those numbers would have been even higher if he did not miss three games.

In the NFC championship game against the Green Bay Packers, Jacobs ran for 67 yards on the frozen tundra at Lambeau Field and scored one major. His most memorable hit came when he sent Packer cornerback Charles Woodson sprawling on a five-yard run. In all, Jacobs ran for 197 yards in the playoffs — including 42 in the Super Bowl upset win over New England — with three scores to help the 10–6 Giants claim a championship by winning four straight games on the road.

IN THE HUDDLE
In 2005 Jacobs became the first Giants rookie to score seven touchdowns since 1984.

Jacobs and the Giants did not rest on their laurels in 2008, earning the NFC's top seed with a 12–4 record. New York's most reliable runner recorded a career-high 1,089 yards and scored 15 touchdowns, also a career best. Jacobs has been helped along the way by an excellent offensive line, and the maturation of quarterback Eli Manning has also been a major factor in New York becoming one of the best teams in the NFL. However, the 2008 season ended in a disappointing manner as Philadelphia held the Giants in check for most of their playoff contest which went to the visiting Eagles, 23–11. Jacobs ran for 92 yards on 19 carries against Philly, but anyone watching the New York club late in the season knew the Giants were in trouble and that a second consecutive trip to the Super Bowl was in doubt.

However, the Giants are still young enough to bounce back and might even become a dynasty if they can keep the key parts of their team together. Jacobs should certainly stay a big part of the Giants' future as the team signed him to a four-year $25-million contract. The contract includes $13 million in guarantees and Jacobs will make $15 million in the first two years of the deal.

CHRIS JOHNSON

Every game Chris Johnson plays in has the potential to erupt into a track meet. His blazing speed has been part of his remarkable repertoire for years, but the tongues started wagging on the pro football front as soon as Johnson was clocked at the NFL draft combine.

He was timed at 4.24 seconds over the 40-yard challenge — the fastest time since the combine went to electronic timing. If the Tennessee Titans, who were looking for explosiveness at running back and on kick returns, needed any further stamp of approval for Johnson, he provided it with his superhero speed that day.

The Titans selected the 5-foot-11, 200-pounder from the East Carolina Pirates 24th overall in the 2008 NFL draft. Johnson and Tulane's Matt Forte (drafted by the Chicago Bears in the second round) were the most highly regarded senior running backs available in the class of 2008, which was full of early-eligible players at that position. In Johnson's case, joining the Titans was a nice coincidence considering he was a standout athlete for the Olympia High School Titans in his native Orlando, Florida.

Believing they landed a special player, the Titans worked at getting Johnson plenty of touches in his rookie season. He responded by rushing for 93 yards on 15 carries and adding 34 yards on three receptions (with one touchdown) in Week 1, a 17–10 win over the Jacksonville Jaguars. By season's

end, Johnson had started 14 of the 15 games he played and rushed for 1,228 yards with nine touchdowns on 251 carries. He also contributed 260 yards on 43 receptions with one TD.

IN THE HUDDLE
Johnson finished fifth in the AFC with 1,488 total yards from scrimmage.

Johnson helped the Titans to the best record in the NFL at 13–3 and then assisted in Tennessee's total offensive domination of the Baltimore Ravens in the post-season. He rushed for 72 yards on 11 carries with one TD and caught one pass for 28 yards against the respected Ravens defense. But errors doomed the Titans, whose Super Bowl quest ended with a 13–10 loss to Baltimore. Johnson had one more game to play, though, as he'd earned a spot in the Pro Bowl. And although he was a distant second, Johnson was runner-up to Atlanta QB Matt Ryan for NFL offensive rookie of the year.

Born on September 23, 1985, Johnson's flair at running back attracted a lot of attention, as did his prowess in basketball and track and field. He developed into a world-class sprinter and his ability to gain a career in pro

football was boosted enormously by his dedication to track.

Running track allowed him to stay fit year-round and, as a running back, it helped fire him out of the backfield like a sprinter out of the starting block. Johnson was clocked at 10.38 seconds in the 100-meter dash, while he also anchored the Golden South and Golden West National Championship 4-x-100-meter relay team.

In high school, Johnson finished second to Walter Dix in the 100-meter event. Dix just happened to win bronze in the 100-meter and 200-meter events at the 2008 Olympic Games in Beijing. Xavier "X-Man" Carter is another elite sprinter Johnson was familiar with, as well as Beijing 400-meter and 4-x-400-meter relay gold medalist

LaShawn Merritt who also calls East Carolina University his alma mater.

Johnson still follows the exploits of those three and he has no regrets about opting for football because his desire all along was to carve out a career in the NFL. As a senior at East Carolina, he was the top collegiate football player with an average of 227.7 all-purpose yards per game. His college career was completed in brilliant fashion with 408 all-purpose yards, including 223 rushing, as the Pirates beat Boise State in the Hawaii Bowl.

As an NFL rookie, Johnson surpassed 100 yards rushing four times with a career-best 168-yard showing in Week 7 against the Kansas City Chiefs. His first 100-plus yard rushing game

CAREER HIGHLIGHTS

- 2008 Pro Bowl selection.
- Johnson's 168 rushing yards against Kansas City in Week 7 of the 2008 season was the second highest total in a single game by a rookie in team history.
- Named rookie of the week twice in 2008: Week 7 and Week 9.

occurred quickly with 109 yards on 19 carries against Cincinnati in Week 2. He also twice scored two touchdowns in one game: Week 4 against the Minnesota Vikings and Week 13 against the Detroit Lions.

Johnson came off the blocks into the NFL the same way he did when running the 100-meter dash; like bolt of lightning.

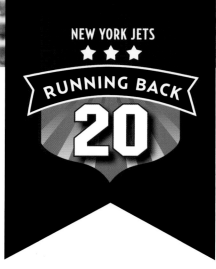

RUNNING BACK
20

THOMAS JONES

CAREER HIGHLIGHTS

• Selected to 2008 Pro Bowl.

• Drafted 7th overall from the University of Virginia by the Arizona Cardinals in 2000.

• Once rushed for 462 yards in a single game as a junior in high school.

Thomas Jones left the Virginia Cavaliers with a school-record 3,998 rushing yards, exactly 609 more than Tiki Barber tabulated during his college career. How could Jones possibly miss as an immediate impact player in the NFL?

The Arizona Cardinals certainly felt he couldn't. After the Baltimore Ravens made Jamal Lewis the first running back to go in the 2000 NFL draft at the No. 5 position, the Cardinals selected Jones two spots later. Three perplexing and injury-hampered seasons with the Cardinals ensued and he was traded to the Tampa Bay Buccaneers in June 2003. It was there he rushed for more than 600 yards for the first time in his NFL career.

Jones then took the free agency route and signed a four-year contract with the Chicago Bears on March 3, 2004. For the next three seasons in the Windy City, Jones blossomed into the useful stud many envisioned in his draft year. He rushed for 948 yards in 2004, a career-high 1,335 yards in 2005 and 1,210 yards in 2006. By going over 1,300 yards in 2005, Jones put himself in royal company, joining Walter Payton as the only two Bears to hit that benchmark. Jones delivered in the post-season of 2006 as well, rushing for 66 yards and two touchdowns in the

divisional playoff win over Seattle and a franchise playoff-record 123 yards (with two TDs) in the NFC championship triumph over New Orleans.

He had plenty left over in Super Bowl XLI, even though the Bears lost 29–17 to the Indianapolis Colts. The Bears rushed only 19 times in the game with Jones getting the call 15 times and amassing 112 yards. But in 2007, the Bears elected to part with Jones and traded him to the New York Jets along with the 63rd pick in that year's draft for a higher position in the second round (37th overall). Chicago's running game struggled in 2007 and only improved a year later with the arrival of rookie Matt Forte. Meanwhile, Jones continued his stellar play for the Jets.

IN THE HUDDLE
Jones has rushed for over 1,000 yards in each of the last four seasons.

Jones rushed for 1,119 yards in 2007 and 1,312 yards in 2008 when he earned a Pro Bowl selection for the first time. His rushing yardage and rushing TDs in 2008 each ranked fifth in the league. His 13 rushing TDs also established a Jets record, as did

the 15 total TDs (two receiving) he scored. In so doing, he surpassed the old marks set by Curtis Martin.

At the end of 2008, the 5-foot-10, 215-pound running back was the recipient of two Jets honors: the Curtis Martin Award as team MVP and the Dennis Byrd Award as most inspirational player.

Thomas, born on August 19, 1978, and his brother Julius, who arrived on August 14, 1981, came from a hard-working family headed by Thomas Sr. and Betty Jones. Their roots — and residence to this day — are in a coal-mining area called Big Stone Gap, Virginia.

Thomas Sr. and Betty both worked the coal mines and the sight of their mother leaving for the overnight shift still makes Thomas Jr. and Julius grateful for lives in pro football.

Thomas Sr. and Betty instilled a deep appreciation of education in their seven children with six already clutching college degrees and the seventh now at the University of Virginia. Thomas Sr. demanded Thomas Jr. and Julius do a series of push-ups and sit-ups every day. The Jones kids used the hills in the region to develop their athletic skills. Thomas Sr. made it a routine to hide the sports pages from his boys

until they'd read other sections of the newspaper and he asked that all his children learn five to 10 new words each day.

Once Thomas Jr. became a pro, he moved his parents out of the small home where they'd raised the family into nicer place in Big Stone Gap. The work ethic Thomas Jones picked up there has served him well as he weathered his early struggles in the NFL to become the player many projected when he turned pro. In 2006, with Julius rushing for the Dallas Cowboys, the two brothers became the NFL's first siblings in the 1,000-yard club in the same season.

JAMAL LEWIS

The enormity of the task at hand didn't deter George Kokinis and Eric Mangini when they became GM and head coach, respectively, of the Cleveland Browns in January 2009. The Browns, almost post-season bound in 2007 with a record of 10–6 for second place in the AFC North, dropped out of sight a year later by finishing 4–12.

The offense showed the eighth-best total in the league with 402 points in 2007, but was tied for second last with the St. Louis Rams in 2008 with a mere 232. Only the Cincinnati Bengals generated fewer with 204.

IN THE HUDDLE
In 2003 Lewis rushed for 2,066 yards, the second most in a season in NFL history.

Kokinis and Mangini did see a bright spot in running back Jamal Lewis, who was born on August 26, 1979. As such, Lewis is older than many running backs out there, especially given the influx of young talent the league has seen. But he keeps producing and his first two seasons with the Browns — after his great numbers with the Baltimore Ravens — are proof of that.

Sixteen players reached 1,000 yards rushing in 2008 and Lewis was No. 16 with 1,002. Seventeen rushers hit 1,000 yards in 2007 and Lewis was No. 5 with 1,304, the most in a season by any Cleveland Brown other than the legendary Jim Brown. By rushing for 94 yards in Week 17 of 2007, Lewis just nosed over the 1,000-yard plateau to become the first Brown since Mike Pruitt to post back-to-back seasons of 1,000-or-more rushing yards (1979–1981). The incentive is there in 2009 for Lewis to take the ball under Mangini's command in an effort to match Pruitt's three consecutive seasons at that standard.

Lewis, who came out of Frederick Douglass High School in his hometown of Atlanta, Georgia, left the University of Tennessee after three years with 2,677 yards rushing (third all-time for the Volunteers) and 3,161 all-purpose yards (fourth all-time at Tennessee). The No. 5 overall selection by the Baltimore Ravens in the 2000 NFL draft then catapulted Lewis into the pro ranks with a rookie season to remember.

The 5-foot-11, 245-pound ball carrier hit 1,364 yards rushing and another 296 yards receiving. In the playoffs, he produced 338 more yards rushing and 40 receiving, making it a total of 2,038 yards with 10 touchdowns — four in the post-season. His seventh game of 100-plus yards rushing in the entire season occurred in Super Bowl XXXV when he galloped to 102 yards on 27 carries with one TD. All Lewis had done in Year 1 of his pro career was join Tony Dorsett as the only NFL rookies to rush for more than 1,000 yards for that season's Super Bowl champion.

CAREER HIGHLIGHTS

- Is the fifth among active NFL running backs in rushing yards with 10,107 yards.
- Named to Pro Bowl in 2003.
- Led the NFL in 2003 with 129.1 rushing yards per game.

The sophomore campaign was a write-off for Lewis after he sustained a knee injury during the first week of training camp. The return to action in 2002 once again saw Lewis breeze by the 1,000-yard rushing mark as he finished with 1,327.

Then Lewis was All-Pro, named to the Pro Bowl team and chosen the AP offensive player of the year in 2003 after rushing for 2,066 yards and a franchise-record 14 TDs. Only Eric Dickerson, with 2,105, had rushed for more yards in a single season and Lewis became the fifth NFLer to strike the 2,000-yard rushing peak behind Buffalo's O.J. Simpson with 2,003 in 1973, Dickerson of the L.A. Rams in 1984, Detroit's Barry Sanders with 2,053 in 1997 and Denver's Terrell Davis with 2,008 in 1998.

Included in Lewis' season was a Week 2 performance against the Browns in which he set the NFL record for most rushing yards in one game with 295 on 30 carries. That standard lasted until Minnesota rookie Adrian Peterson rushed for 296 yards on 30 carries against San Diego on November 4, 2007.

Lewis posted 1,006 rushing yards over 12 games in 2004 with the four games he missed due to a league-imposed suspension. Lewis plead guilty to a sting operation for his part in trying to set up a drug deal dating back to 2000. Aside from the NFL suspension, Lewis served four months in prison during the off-season after 2004. Once back in 2005, he rushed for 906 yards over 15 games then was back over 1,000 yards by accumulating 1,132 in 2006. Released by the Ravens in 2007, Lewis headed for the Dog Pound where he's shown 1,000-yard seasons are still his domain.

MARSHAWN LYNCH

CAREER HIGHLIGHTS

• In Week 9 of the 2007 NFL season, Lynch threw an eight-yard touchdown pass to tight end Robert Royal.

• Has back-to-back 1,000-yard rushing seasons (2007, 2008).

• Was awarded co-offensive player of the game versus Texas A&M in the 2007 Holiday Bowl.

As a rookie in 2007, Buffalo Bills running back Marshawn Lynch had a very good season despite the fact he missed three games with a high ankle sprain. His performance could be best described as solid, racking up 1,115 yards on 280 running attempts for a 4.0 per-carry average. It was the first time a Bills rookie running back had gained more than 1,000 yards along the ground since Greg Bell in 1984. At times his play was great to watch as Lynch took on the first line of tacklers and just kept churning his legs until he ground out more yardage. His determination to break into the open was all the more impressive when it was clear defenses were keying on him. Lynch was also very capable of breaking off a long run at anytime, but the Bills were not a strong team and finished a disappointing 7–9 and out of the playoffs once again.

A native of Oakland, California, Lynch was a very good athlete in his high school days. He excelled as a running back at Oakland Technical High School and gained 1,772 yards rushing and scored 23 TDs in just eight games in 2003. Lynch also played defensive back as a senior — picking off 20 enemy passes — and he even tried his hand as a defensive end. Lynch also played basketball and was a sprinter in track and field. He chose to attend the University of California and in his second season with the Golden Bears, Lynch ran for 1,246 yards and scored 10 majors. He was named MVP of the Las Vegas Bowl by scoring three touchdowns and rushing for 194 yards. By the time his college career was coming to an end (he skipped his senior season), Lynch was one of the top players in the country and was considered a Heisman Trophy candidate. The university tried to hype Lynch for the prestigious award by putting together highlights of his best performances from 2004 to 2006, but quarterback Troy Smith of Ohio State took the award. Lynch finished his college career with 1,356 yards rushing and 11 touchdowns in 2006.

The Bills selected Lynch 12th overall in the first round of the 2007 NFL draft and he joined their lineup as a starter right from the beginning. Buffalo had said good-bye to running back Willis McGahee by trading him to Baltimore and felt strongly Lynch could take his place. After his solid rookie campaign the Bills naturally expected more from Lynch in 2008. At times he delivered, but he played two more games than his rookie year and ended with slightly fewer yards, posting 1,036 on 250 carries for a 4.1 yards-per-carry average. Buffalo started the 2008 season strongly with five wins in its first six games. Lynch's best effort over that time came in the form of 83 yards against the Oakland Raiders, a game that was played in Lynch's hometown. Lynch did not post a 100-yard contest along the ground until he ran for 119 yards against Cleveland in the middle of November. He also had 134 yards against San Francisco and 127 versus the New York Jets, but the Bills lost all three games in which Lynch put up 100 or more yards. On the more positive side, he caught 47 passes out of the backfield and totaled nine touchdowns on the season. The Bills also got Lynch some help in the backfield by using Fred Jackson (an undrafted free agent signed in 2007) more often. Jackson chipped in with 571 yards rushing with an impressive 4.4 yards per carry. The duo could be a very effective combination for Buffalo over the next few seasons.

IN THE HUDDLE

Lynch has only fumbled the ball three times in 530 rushing attempts.

If Lynch is to fully tap into his potential, he must become more mature as a person and make better decisions. In 2008 he was charged for leaving the scene of an accident in which a pedestrian was injured, with Lynch claiming he did not know his car had hit anyone. A plea was worked out and he was not suspended by the NFL for that indiscretion, but in January of 2009, he was charged with weapons possession in California. The NFL suspended Lynch for the first three games of the 2009 season for violating the league's personal conduct policy. Lynch was very apologetic and said the suspension was a wake-up call. It will be interesting to see how Lynch will respond to his suspension both on and off the field. His career may depend on it.

MINNESOTA VIKINGS

RUNNING BACK
28

ADRIAN
PETERSON

Minnesota Vikings running back Adrian Peterson is a very ambitious person. To understand why he is this way one has to closely look at his upbringing, which was filled with triumph and tragedy.

When he was seven years old, Adrian saw his older brother Brian die after he was hit by a drunk driver while riding his bike. As if that wasn't enough, his father, Nelson, who introduced Adrian to football, was sent to prison for laundering drug money when the youngster was just 12 years of age. Peterson was

never bitter towards his father, although he missed his day-to-day influence terribly. As he reached high school age, Peterson did not always hang out with a great crowd and trouble always seemed to be around. His mother, Bonita, basically raised Peterson alone and she gave him values to live by, including goals like getting good grades and being the best he could possibly be all the time. Peterson was trying his best to live up to his mother's lofty objectives, but it took a phone call from his still-incarcerated father to get him back on the

right track; in that call Nelson told his son he had what it took to be the best running back in all of Texas. The very clear message seemed to snap Peterson to attention and in his junior year at Palestine High School his performance was so impressive he became the most recruited player in the country. By his senior season, Peterson rushed for 2,960 yards and scored 32 touchdowns. He attended Oklahoma and set an NCAA record for first-year players when he carried the ball for 1,925 yards. After his junior year Peterson made himself

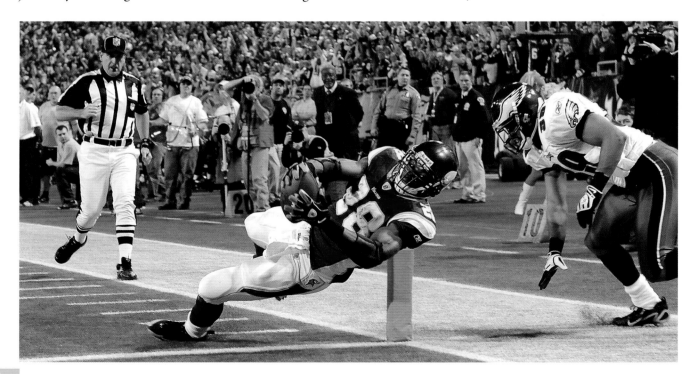

eligible for the 2007 NFL draft and the Vikings were very lucky to grab him with the seventh pick.

IN THE HUDDLE

Peterson led the NFL in average rushing yards per game with a 95.8-yard average in 2007 and a whopping 110-yard average in 2008.

Peterson's athletic skills came from his parents — his father was a good basketball player and his mother a track and field performer — and they were also able to instill a special will to succeed in their son. He took the NFL by storm in his first season by rushing for 1,341 yards on 268 carries. That represented the NFL's second-highest total in 2007, despite the fact he missed two games. Peterson set a league record with a 296-yard effort against the San Diego Chargers on November 4. He won all the rookie of the year awards associated with the NFL and was named MVP of the Pro Bowl when he rushed for 129 yards and scored two touchdowns. Despite all this, the Vikings were only able to post an 8–8 record and missed the post-season.

As hard as it is to believe, Peterson was actually better in 2008 when he led the entire NFL in rushing with 1,760 yards and the Vikings were back in the playoffs with an NFC North-best record of 10–6. The fun ended there, though, as the Philadelphia Eagles beat the Vikings in Minnesota during the first weekend of the playoffs. The visitors were able to hold Peterson to just 83 yards on 20 carries.

Although he is very skilled, Peterson quickly recognized the pro game was very different than college. When he attended Oklahoma he would just take the

ball and run as fast as he could. Upon joining the Vikings, he had to learn about how to pick his way through some very tough and smart defenders. He had to learn to let his offensive linemen do their job first before he could do his.

Peterson was a very quick study and able to grasp the varied duties he had as a running back. In his two NFL seasons to date, Peterson has also impressed by what he does without the ball. He runs good routes and can step up to block when called upon. He can gain yards by running inside and is extremely dangerous if he can get outside. He is always a threat to break for a long run anytime his is given the ball. The Vikings would be wise

CAREER HIGHLIGHTS

- Won the NFL rushing title in 2008 with 1,760 yards on 363 carries.
- Two-time Pro Bowl Selection (2007, 2008).
- 2007 Pro Bowl MVP.
- Was named the 2007 AP offensive rookie of the year.

involve him more on pass plays because the 6-foot-1, 217-pounder is a good receiver and he can make solo tacklers look foolish trying to bring him down. Peterson's one weakness may be that he tends to run while his body is too vertical, which makes him an easy target for the tacklers who can actually get their hands on him.

CLINTON PORTIS

Running back Clinton Portis knew he faced some obstacles when he came out of the University of Miami in 2002. He was listed at 5-foot-11 and 195 pounds and many scouts believed he would be too small to play in the NFL. The Denver Broncos took a chance and selected Portis in the second round of the 2002 draft, 51st overall, hoping he would be able to bring a winning attitude to Denver since he had been in such a successful program in Miami, where the Hurricanes had an undefeated season in 2001 to win the national championship. In addition to the size issue, Portis was well aware people wondered about his work habits, questionable hands and whether he would be there when the game was on the line.

IN THE HUDDLE
Portis was named the 2002 AP offensive rookie of the year.

Portis erased all doubts when he scored 15 touchdowns in his rookie year while running for 1,508 yards for the Broncos. He also caught another 33 passes in 2002, but Denver missed the playoffs with a 9–7 record. In 2003 he topped his first-year mark by rushing for 1,591 yards — still his career-best total — and hauled in 38 passes helping the Broncos get to the playoffs with a 10–6 record. Portis had clearly established himself as one of the best backs in the NFL and wanted to be paid that way when it was time to work out a new deal. When Portis told the Broncos how much money he was looking for, they gave him and his agent the opportunity to shop around the league for a taker. The Washington Redskins showed strong interest and sent all-star cornerback Champ Bailey to Denver along with a second round draft choice to get Portis' rights. Washington gave Portis an eight-year deal worth $50 million — quite a reward for a player with only two years of experience.

Portis had a fair showing in his first season as a Redskin, but the 2004 Washington team was only 6–10 and people began to question the deal that brought him to town. Sensitive to what the critics were saying, Portis withdrew somewhat and decided all his talking would be done on the football field. He was stellar in 2005 with 1,515 yards along the ground for 11 touchdowns, a performance that helped the Redskins get into the playoffs with a 10–6 mark. Portis experienced his first playoff victory against Tampa Bay, but lost to Seattle the following week. Injured for half of the 2006 season, Portis proved resilient when he rushed for 1,262 yards in 2007 and a

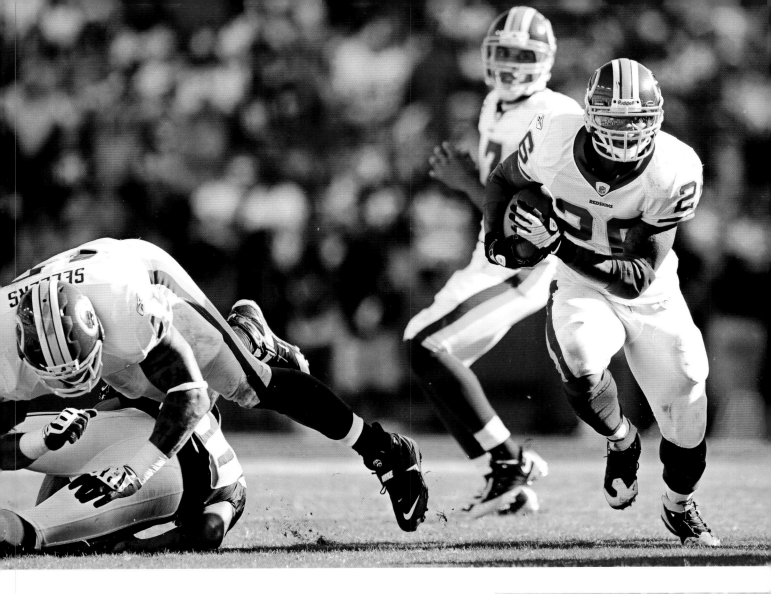

playoff berth with a 9–7 mark in Joe Gibbs' last season as the Redskins head coach.

Portis is a bit of an odd character off the field to say the least. Former teammates at Miami said he was quite a comedian and enjoyed pulling pranks. But he took it one step further when he joined the Redskins by buying costumes and creating his own characters, much the same way as one of his main comedic influences, Flip Wilson, used to do on *The Flip Wilson Show*. Portis created at least five different characters and fans began to send him other costume ideas. He decided to mothball his acts because the attention they garnered was becoming too much for him to handle. Another incident with

far graver consequences also had a huge affect on Portis.

When teammate Sean Taylor, a player Portis was very close to, was shot and killed during a robbery attempt at his home, the running back began to think more about his life and where he was going. Taylor's death made him realize everything could be gone in an instant and he rededicated himself to the game to honor his late friend, working hard in the off-season to prepare for the 2008 campaign.

Portis played in all 16 games, running for 1,487 yards while showing a strong determination that served as a great example for all his teammates and coaches. He wanted the ball in key situations and new coach Jim Zorn saw a gritty

CAREER HIGHLIGHTS

• Two-time Pro Bowl selection (2003, 2008).

• Rushed for over 3,000 yards in his first two NFL seasons with the Denver Broncos.

• Is fourth among active players with 72 rushing touchdowns.

performance by his star runner, who pushed and pulled for every yard he gained. A hot start for the Redskins ended badly with four losses in their last five games to give them an 8–8 record on the year. However, Portis showed he could run with a purpose and also became a devastating blocker in the Redskins backfield.

STEVE SLATON

HOUSTON TEXANS

RUNNING BACK 20

It's one thing for a rookie to burst onto the scene, but it's how that freshman performs over the long term and particularly at the finish line that determines whether the kid really has what it takes. Running back Steve Slaton of the Houston Texans showed his true colors throughout 2008, putting in a terrific campaign and flourishing in his first NFL start during a loss in Week 3 at Tennessee with 116 yards on 18 carries and one touchdown.

Slaton posted a career-high 156-yard dazzler of a game that included a 71-yard romp for a TD in a defeat at Indianapolis in Week 11, and he continued to shift his game to a higher gear down the stretch. From Week 13 on Slaton was devastating: he rushed for 130 yards on 21 carries with two TDs while catching two passes for 52 yards in a win over Jacksonville; rushed for 120 yards on 26 attempts in a victory at Green Bay; ran for 100 yards on 24 attempts in a triumph over Tennessee; gained 66 yards on 18 carries in a loss at Oakland and rushed for 92 yards on 20 carries along with one TD in the season-ending win over Chicago.

The Texans completed 2008 on a 4–1 run with Slaton's 508

yards ranking second in the league for that period. Add his passing yardage totals to the mix and his combined 687 yards for that stretch topped the NFL. His phenomenal play netted him the NFL rookie of the month nod for December.

IN THE HUDDLE

Slaton's 1,282 rushing yards is the fifth-highest this decade among rookies.

Slaton became the second 1,000-yard rusher for the Texans and established a single-season franchise record with 1,282 yards rushing, surpassing the total of 1,188 set by Domanick Williams in 2004. Slaton was the leading NFL rusher among rookies in 2008 and sixth when mixed in with the veterans. Showing his brilliant breakaway capabilities, he equaled DeAngelo Williams of the Carolina Panthers for the NFL lead with five runs of 40-plus yards and was tied for third with Clinton Portis of the Washington Redskins with 13 dashes of 20-or-more yards.

At 5-foot-9 and 203 pounds Slaton is a compact player who knows how to find holes and follow blocking. He isn't short on confidence and he fits right

CAREER HIGHLIGHTS

- Led all rookies with five 100-plus-yard rushing games including three consecutive 100-plus-yard rushing games (Week 13–15).
- AFC offensive player of the week for Week 14 of the 2008 season.
- Accounted for 27 percent of Houston's franchise-record 6,113 yards from scrimmage.

in with the Texans and their newfound bravado. Given their 8–8 records in 2007 and 2008 the Texans won't be taken lightly any longer. And they relish the thought of center stage. That was evident with how they handled their Week 13 debut on *Monday Night Football*. They knew the world was watching and they were ready to put on a show. Slaton told head coach Gary Kubiak to count on him and give him the ball. Kubiak did and Slaton didn't let him down.

Steve was born to Carl Slaton and Juanita Tiggett-Slaton in Levittown, Pennsylvania, on January 4, 1986. He was the sixth child in the combined family consisting of Carl's four kids and Juanita's one from previous relationships. Steve dealt with a hearing impediment that was finally corrected by the time he was in Grade 1 and then reconciled the passing of one of his sisters to leukemia four years later.

He was a natural in football and track while at Conwell-Egan Catholic High School in Fairless Hills, Pennsylvania. His football ability attracted broad interest and he had his mind set on attending Maryland, only to be heartbroken when that school took away its original offer. So he went to West Virginia and became a terrific recruit for the Mountaineers.

In three years, he rushed for the third-best total in West Virginia history with 3,923 yards, but his 50 TDs via the rush rank first for the Mountaineers. He provided a highlight reel performance at the 2006 Sugar Bowl with 204 yards rushing against Georgia, the second highest total in a Bowl Championship Series clash.

Forgoing his senior year, Slaton went into the 2008 NFL draft, where he was the 10th running back chosen when Houston picked him in the third round, 89th overall. That same year, Slaton was joined by Chicago's Matt Forte and Tennessee's Chris Johnson in tying an NFL record as the trio of rookies each ran 1,000-or-more yards in one season.

Slaton reminds Kubiak of Portis. That's a nice comparison for a young man making a name for himself in Houston.

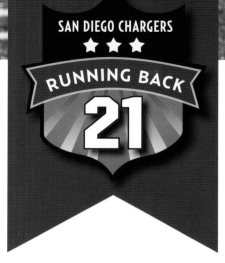

LADAINIAN TOMLINSON

The 2008 NFL season was not exactly the best of times for San Diego Chargers running back LaDainian Tomlinson. The star all-purpose back did not perform nearly as well as he had in the past and began to question whether, at the age of 30, he could take the pounding of a full season. He has found it difficult to stay healthy enough to play up to his capabilities, although he rarely misses a regular season game. Tomlinson has been plagued by knee, toe and groin injuries over the years. With San Diego's offense increasingly being built around quarterback Philip Rivers' passing abilities, Tomlinson's role has been a bit reduced. But he is a good team player who would not create controversy over the way he was used by head coach Norv Turner. The San Diego Chargers are the only NFL club the gifted back has played for, and Tomlinson wants to retire as a Charger. However, concerns about his contract affecting the team's salary cap may force both parties to rethink their relationship for the 2009 season and beyond.

To say Tomlinson has been a star since he entered the NFL would be something of an understatement. After a superb college career at Texas Christian University, the 5-foot-10, 221-pound running back was still considered a bit of a risk because of his size. Tomlinson was able to prove he was a good inside runner over his final seasons at Texas Christian, which made him a Heisman Trophy finalist and a consensus top-10 choice going into the 2001 NFL draft. The Chargers actually held the first overall selection and

coveted quarterback Michael Vick, but could not reach a contract agreement with the pivot. A trade was made with Atlanta, which selected Vick, and the Chargers took Tomlinson with the Falcons' original fifth selection. It was a choice the Chargers would never regret and to show how pleased they were to get him, San Diego management gave Tomlinson a six-year deal valued at $38 million.

IN THE HUDDLE
Tomlinson holds the all-time NFL record for single-season rushing touchdowns with 28.

Tomlinson paid immediate dividends by rushing for 1,236 yards as a rookie, scoring 10 times along the ground and catching 59 passes for 367 yards. The next two seasons saw him record over 1,600 yards rushing each year and he also made 179 catches and scored a total of 32 touchdowns. His statistics slipped somewhat in 2004, but he regained his from in 2005, which was just a taste of what Tomlinson's 2006 campaign delivered. His performance that season was one of the best by a running back in NFL history. Tomlinson set a league record by scoring 31 touchdowns (28 along the ground and three on pass receptions for a total of

186 points scored — also an NFL single-season record) while rushing for 1,815 yards (for a 5.2 yards per carry average) and added another 508 yards to the Chargers offense with 56 catches to his credit. His outstanding performance in 2006 was recognized when he was named the MVP of the NFL — the first time a Charger was so recognized. San Diego had an NFL-best 14–2 record in 2006, but was knocked off at home in the playoffs by the New England Patriots 24–21. The 2007 season saw the Chargers win 11 games and get to the AFC championship game, but the Patriots beat them again 21–12 to end their Super Bowl hopes. Tomlinson contributed 1,474 yards rushing and he scored a total of 18 touchdowns

in 2007, but it seems like no matter what the talented runner does, it's never enough to get the Chargers over the hump.

Tomlinson has done so well as an NFL player because he is very dedicated to his job. He takes weightlifting very seriously and works on his core by doing balance-specific exercises. He has breakaway speed when he gets into the open and his powerful physique allows him to pound the ball inside between tackles. Tomlinson gets into the right positions because he understands the game so well and he makes tough plays look rather easy. He is also a good blocker when needed and is considered an excellent team leader. A running back can expect

CAREER HIGHLIGHTS

- His streak of 18 consecutive games rushing for a touchdown between 2004–2005 set an NFL record.

- Has led the NFL in rushing TDs tree times in his career (2004, 2006, 2007) and rushing yards twice (2006, 2007).

- Leads all active players in yards from scrimmage with 15,561 yards.

to see some decline as they get older, especially one who has been used as much as Tomlinson with the Chargers. If he can find a way to overcome his nagging injuries, Tomlinson should be good for a few more years of high-quality play.

ATLANTA FALCONS
RUNNING BACK
33

MICHAEL TURNER

When Atlanta Falcons GM Thomas Dimitroff and head coach Mike Smith welcomed running back Michael Turner to the fold with a six-year contract carrying a stipend of $34.5 million, they talked about acquiring a quality player and person ready to take the next step.

It didn't take long to find out that the assessment was bang on. Turner, stepping into the limelight after four seasons as the understudy to LaDainian Tomlinson with the San Diego Chargers, set the Falcons single-game rushing record in Week 1 of 2008. He churned out 220 yards rushing, including a 66-yard TD run, on 22 attempts in Atlanta's 34–21 win over the Detroit Lions.

IN THE HUDDLE
Turner's average of 4.9 yards per rushing attempt ranks him fifth among all active NFLers.

He bookended that performance in Week 17 when he rushed for 208 yards on 25 carries with one TD in a 31–27 decision over the St. Louis Rams. On the season, the 5-foot-10, 244-pounder from Waukegan, Illinois, produced eight games with more than 100 yards rushing.

Turner was a first-time selection to the All-Pro Team and the Pro Bowl after finishing second in the NFL — and establishing Falcons records — with 1,699 yards rushing and 17 rushing TDs. His 376 rushing attempts ranked first in the

NFL. During his time with San Diego, Turner started once in 59 regular season games. His stats line showed 1,257 yards rushing from 228 attempts, with six touchdowns.

The Chargers appeared on their way to trading Turner as a restricted free agent during the 2007 off-season, but held on to him for one more year. When he became an unrestricted free agent after 2007, Turner tested the market and found his niche with the rebuilding Falcons. Atlanta's big step forward in 2008 got the team to the post-season, where the Cardinals stuck the Falcons with a 30–24 wild card defeat in Arizona. Turner was held to 42 yards on 18 carries in that game, so the Cardinals' defense deserves credit for finding a way to halt this force from the backfield.

Born on February 13, 1982, Turner's path to the NFL took him through North Chicago High School, where he was offensive player of the year and MVP as a junior and senior. He has a penchant for making terrific first impressions and did so in college by racking up 238 yards rushing in his first contest with Northern Illinois University. By the time he left NIU, his 4,941 yards rushing ranked 13th all-time in NCAA annals.

CAREER HIGHLIGHTS

- Was second in rushing yards in 2008 with 1,699 yards.
- Finished second in average yards per game in 2008 with a mark of 106.2 yards.
- Was tied for second in MVP voting in 2008.
- Pro Bowl and All-Pro selection in 2008.

The Chargers drafted Turner in 2004 with the 154th overall selection in the fifth round. He started his first — and as it turned out, only — game with the Chargers in final contest of 2004, tallying 87 yards on 15 attempts. One of the moments that defined his vast potential occurred during Week 15 in 2005 when the Chargers visited the unbeaten Indianapolis Colts. Turner came off the bench after Tomlinson bruised a knee and supplied 113 yards rushing on eight attempts, highlighted by an 83-yard TD scamper. The Chargers beat the Colts 26–17 in what was one of a few occasions that Turner would sub effectively for the injured Tomlinson.

In Week 2 of 2006, a big win over the Tennessee Titans saw Tomlinson (19 attempts for 71 yards and two TDs) and Turner (13 carries for 138 yards) share the load. A season later in another lopsided game during Week 5 at Denver, the LT–MT combo got ample time again with Tomlinson rushing 21 times for 67 yards, while Turner had 10 carries for 147 yards.

Tomlinson made headlines in the 2007 post-season when injuries limited his playing time. Turner relieved Tomlinson in the wild card win over Tennessee with 28 yards rushing on nine attempts. He then delivered big time once more in Indianapolis with 17 carries for 71 yards as the Chargers shocked the Colts 28–24 in the divisional playoffs. The Patriots, however, were too much to overcome in the AFC championship, winning 21–12 while holding Tomlinson to five yards on his two rushes in brief playing time, while Turner added 65 yards on 17 attempts.

The first Tomlinson–Turner head-to-head matchup occurred in Week 13 of 2008 when the Falcons won a pivotal game in their playoff drive, 22–16 at San Diego. The Falcons defense kept Tomlinson in check as he only had 24 yards on 14 attempts, while San Diego couldn't find an answer for Turner, as he put up 120 yards on 31 carries with one TD.

PHILADELPHIA EAGLES
★ ★ ★
RUNNING BACK
36

BRIAN WESTBROOK

When the Philadelphia Eagles signed running back Brian Westbrook to a new six-year contract prior to the start of the 2008 season, management said all the right things about one of the best players in team history. Coach Andy Reid said Westbrook was the best back in football, able to do everything out of the backfield including catching, blocking and running. Team president Joe Banner said Westbrook was a future Hall of Fame player and his new contract reflected his status as one of the best players in the NFL. Banner went on to say Westbrook was a team leader who wanted to win very badly. It was a very accurate description of a player who has shown his character on many occasions, one of which stands out above all the others.

Westbrook had his finest NFL season in 2007, when he rushed for 1,333 yards, caught 90 passes out of the backfield for 771 yards and scored a total of 14 touchdowns — and he could have scored a 15th major when the Eagles were playing the Dallas Cowboys on December 16, 2007.

The Eagles were in front protecting a 10–6 lead with 2:50 remaining when Cowboy QB Tony Romo threw his third interception of the contest. The

Eagles drove down the field and secured a first down at the Dallas 25-yard line with 2:19 left on the clock. Westbrook took a hand-off on the ensuing play and burst into the clear. As he headed for the Cowboys end zone it looked like he would score an easy touchdown. Instead Westbrook downed himself at the one-yard line. The play ended with the two-minute warning and the Cowboys were out of timeouts. With a fresh set of downs all Philadelphia quarterback Donovan McNabb

had to do was run down the clock. By Westbrook not taking the touchdown and the Eagles not going for a final score, there was no chance for Dallas to regain possession of the ball in order to make a miracle play to win the game. Not many players would have passed on a chance to score the easy touchdown, but Westbrook is not like most players.

Westbrook first joined the Eagles after they selected him 91st overall in the 2002 NFL draft. He starred at Villanova

University, where he rushed for more than 1,000 yards three times. Westbrook racked up 2,823 all-purpose yards over his entire college career and his senior year saw him score 29 touchdowns — 22 running, six on pass receptions and one on a kickoff return. He may have lasted as long as he did in the draft because at 5-foot-10 and 205 pounds, he is not the biggest back in the world, nor did he play for a school that is considered a major football program.

IN THE HUDDLE
Westbrook led the NFL in yards from scrimmage in 2007 with 2,104 yards.

He started slowly with the Eagles, mostly playing on special teams, and excelled as a kick returner. Westbrook took two punts all the way back for touchdowns in 2003. He showed flashes of his running ability when he was given an opportunity, but never reached the 1,000-yard mark. His per-carry average, however, was never below 4.0. Westbrook was also a favorite target coming out of the backfield with 73 catches in 2004 and 61 receptions in 2005. The 2004 season saw Westbrook become a starter for the first time (12 games) and that helped the Eagles make it to the Super Bowl, where they lost 24–21 to New England despite his touchdown catch.

In 2006 and 2007, Westbrook was handed the ball a total of 518 times and he totaled 2,250 yards along the ground. Proving he was very much a multiple threat, Westbrook also caught 167 passes over those two years for 1,440 yards and had 23 combined TDs over the same time frame. Because he doesn't have a huge frame, Westbrook

has taken a beating to achieve his great numbers. Luckily, he has a strong lower body that allows him to break many tackles. He has many good moves that can leave tacklers grasping at air and often it takes more than one defender to bring him down.

The 2008 season was up and down for both Westbrook and the Eagles. The running back had nagging injuries bothering him all year and although he managed to play 14 games, he missed the 1,000-yard mark in rushing for the first time in four seasons,

CAREER HIGHLIGHTS
- Two-time Pro Bowl selection (2004, 2007).
- In 2007 rushed for 1,333 yards, third most in the NFL.
- The average length of his 29 career regular-season touchdowns is 21.3 yards.

finishing with 936. To ensure Westbrook plays longer, the Eagles will have to get the ball to other backs and lighten the load on their star performer.

RECEIVERS

ANQUAN BOLDIN — Arizona Cardinals

CHRIS COOLEY — Washington Redskins

LARRY FITZGERALD — Arizona Cardinals

ANTONIO GATES — San Diego Chargers

TONY GONZALEZ — Atlanta Falcons

SANTONIO HOLMES — Pittsburgh Steelers

T.J. HOUSHMANDZADEH — Seattle Seahawks

ANDRE JOHNSON — Houston Texans

CALVIN JOHNSON — Detroit Lions

BRANDON MARSHALL — Denver Broncos

RANDY MOSS — New England Patriots

STEVE SMITH — Carolina Panthers

HINES WARD — Pittsburgh Steelers

REGGIE WAYNE — Indianapolis Colts

WES WELKER — New England Patriots

RODDY WHITE — Atlanta Falcons

JASON WITTEN — Dallas Cowboys

ANQUAN BOLDIN

It was not surprising to see Arizona Cardinals wide receiver Anquan Boldin stay down on the turf after he was absolutely whacked by New York Jets safeties Kerry Rhodes and Eric Smith. It was something of an unnecessary collision since the game had only 27 seconds left and the Jets were comfortably out in front by a 56–27 count.

Boldin, one of the toughest receivers in the league, took a hit from behind by Rhodes and then another from the front by Smith, who would be suspended for one game and fined $50,000 for his helmet-to-helmet attack. Boldin was carried off the field on a stretcher, but luckily he was able to move all his extremities. He did, however, sustain a fracture to his sinuses along with a swollen face and cut lip. It was the hardest hit Boldin has endured since he entered the NFL, but he took in stride, healed and returned to the Cardinals lineup after missing three weeks. In that game against the Jets, Boldin made 10 receptions for 119 yards and one touchdown, giving him 27 catches for 366 yards after just four weeks of the 2008 season. He returned to play in late October and caught nine passes for 63 yards and two touchdowns against Carolina to show he was not going to change one bit. He went on to make 89 catches in 2008, good for 1,038 yards and 11 touchdowns.

Boldin came to the Cardinals after a college career at Florida State. The 6-foot-1, 217-pounder was considered very athletic and known for his work ethic. These attributes helped make Boldin the 22nd pick of the 2003 NFL draft, although some experts were concerned about his speed at the professional level. However, Boldin adjusted beautifully, recording ten catches for 217 yards against Detroit in his first-ever NFL contest. His immediate impact got him noticed throughout the league, but he was still able to make 101 catches for 1,377 yards and eight touchdowns.

IN THE HUDDLE
Boldin became the fastest player in NFL history to reach 400 career receptions.

His second season saw him play in only 10 games, but he came back in 2005 to record career highs in receptions (102) and receiving yards (1,402). Boldin has not caught 100 passes in one campaign since then, but has recorded seasons of 83, 79 and 89 catches the last three years to establish himself as one of the most consistent players in the NFL.

Boldin is known for playing a physical style and he likes it that way. Opponents have commented on the fact Boldin likes to run over people and acts more like a running back than a receiver. Boldin has a solid build and does not go down easily when he is being tackled, instead fighting for every yard no matter what the situation. The Cardinals like to get the ball out quickly to Boldin and then let him do his thing in the open field. Arizona has also used him as a runner on occasion

CAREER HIGHLIGHTS

- Became the third-fastest player in NFL history to reach the 4,000-yard receiving mark.

- Three-time Pro Bowl selection (2003, 2006, 2008).

- Currently holds the NFL active and career record for receiving yards per game with 81.2 yards.

- Was the only rookie selected to the Pro Bowl in 2003.

and Boldin does not see himself as just a receiver, but, as he is inclined to put it, a football player. Never afraid to speak up when needed, Boldin openly argued with offensive coordinator Todd Haley (now head coach of the Kansas City Chiefs) in plain view of TV cameras. The feisty receiver just had to let his coach know he wanted to be involved in the plays when it mattered most.

Boldin also let be known he was unhappy with his contractual situation during training camp prior to the start of the 2008 season. His current deal runs through the 2010 season, but you can bet he came to attention when fellow wide receiver Larry Fitzgerald

signed his $40-million deal with the Cardinals.

Before he acts too hastily and demands a trade, Boldin might stop to consider he is much more effective with Fitzgerald on the other side taking up the attention of many defenders. That was certainly the case for most of the 2009 Super Bowl, when the Pittsburgh Steelers focused on shutting down Fitzgerald and left Boldin open for eight catches and 84 yards. Although Boldin did not have the spectacular results of Fitzgerald in the 2008 post-season, he did contribute 14 receptions for 190 yards as the Cardinals made it to the league's championship game for the first time in team history.

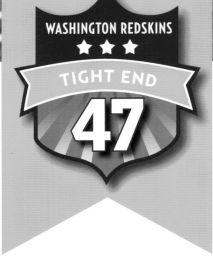

CHRIS COOLEY

Whether it's his name (Cooley), his nickname (Captain Chaos), his hairstyles, his musical tastes ('80s hair band/heavy metal), his love of fantasy football, his outspoken web site/blogs/postings (check out *The Cooley Zone*) or his all-out football talent, colorful Chris Cooley has attracted quite a following. The sure-handed tight end for the Washington Redskins is a fan favorite because he doesn't mind expressing himself.

His No. 47 jersey with "COOLEY" emblazoned on the back is a best seller. His dating of Redskins cheerleader Christy Oglevee went against team policy and that led to her dismissal. No problem; Cooley married her in May 2008. The sky is the limit as to what lies ahead for this extrovert who's risen in his playing class to merit an All-Pro selection in 2005 along with Pro Bowl credentials in 2006 (alternate), 2007 and 2008.

Cooley hails from the small town of Powell, Wyoming, where he was born on July 11, 1982. He left his birthplace at the age of 10 and took up residence in the much-larger Logan, Utah, which had about 33,000 inhabitants in the early 1990s. In Powell and then Logan, Cooley and his younger brother, Tanner, were into a myriad of sports. Chris eventually earned all-state honors as a tight end for Logan High School at the same time he was also establishing himself with letters in baseball and wrestling. Cooley was a state-champion wrestler in his senior year, putting up a record 38 pins in the process of winning all 54 of his matches. He attributes much of what he's accomplished in other sporting pursuits to wrestling, a sport of strength in mind and body.

He went on to star at tight end for the Utah State Aggies, where in his senior year he led the nation's tight ends with 62 catches for 732

CAREER HIGHLIGHTS

- Drafted 81st overall from Utah State University by the Washington Redskins in 2004.
- Ranks as the second most prolific tight end in Redskins team history with 314 receptions, 3,457 receiving yards and 28 touchdowns.
- Has played in the Pro Bowl twice (2007, 2008).
- Led the Redskins in receptions (66) and touchdown receptions (8) in 2007.

yards and six touchdowns. At the 2004 NFL draft, the Redskins selected Cooley in the third round, 81st overall.

Suddenly the wide-eyed kid from Wyoming via Utah had attained his dream of making it as a pro football player, although his entry into the NFL began slowly. Cooley started nine of 16 games for the Redskins in his rookie season of 2004 and managed to score six TDs. His first TD as a pro was a two-yard toss from Mark Brunell at Giants Stadium in Week 2.

Through his first four NFL seasons, Cooley became a go-to option in the Washington attack as he put up six, seven, six and eight TD receptions over his first four years. He set career highs with 83 receptions — also a Redskins franchise record for tight ends — and 849 yards in 2008, but only crossed the goal line once. But his popularity has not waned nor has his importance in Washington's future, even with the arrival in 2008 of USC tight end Fred Davis. The Skins need to upgrade their production in the red zone and Cooley should be a big key in that happening.

IN THE HUDDLE

Cooley's eight touchdown receptions in 2007 marked the first time a tight end led the Redskins in touchdown receptions since Jerry Smith had nine in 1970.

Cooley's failure to score will also hurt his fantasy football value, although on one occasion when he did score three TDs in a game — against Dallas during Week 15 in 2005 — he lost his own fantasy battle on points that week because his opponent had selected him!

His legion of fans can always catch his views on things through his web site and blog. Ably assisted by his brother, Cooley went the blog route as a means of reaching out and having fun. One of his postings on September 14, 2008 was a photo he had taken of some pre-game notes. What he didn't realize was that the posting also showed his private parts.

While the posting remained up all day, it was removed when noticed with an apology for its accidental appearance. Chalk it up as a learning experience for a guy who's in-tune with today's communication network and anxious to keep in touch with his fans. He's even participated in a commercial where he catches a football after punching out behind a piece of drywall.

From his roots in Wyoming throughout his youth and now in the pro ranks, life has never been dull for Cooley nor will it ever be. He's got opinions and he's more than willing to share them. Above all, though, he's one of the game's finest tight ends.

LARRY FITZGERALD

The camera focused in on wide receiver Larry Fitzgerald as a touchdown by the Pittsburgh Steelers was being reviewed. Fitzgerald shook his head and mouthed the words "no, no, no," but sadly for him and the rest of the Arizona Cardinals the score stood and the Steelers hung on for a 27–23 Super Bowl victory.

Just a few minutes earlier, Fitzgerald had connected with Cardinals quarterback Kurt Warner on a 64-yard pass-and-run play to give Arizona a 23–20 lead. Fitzgerald took a pass in the middle of the field and turned on the jets to leave the Steeler defenders huffing and puffing for air as he glided effortlessly into the end zone. Pittsburgh had set out to keep Fitzgerald in check and had done so for most of Super Bowl XLIII by effectively disguising their coverage schemes and assigning two defenders specifically to him. But in the final 11 minutes, he caught six passes for 115 yards and two touchdowns — his first score was a one-yard leaping grab — to give the Cardinals a chance at glory. Fitzgerald demonstrated that, like the great performers before him, he saved his best stuff for the biggest game.

Fitzgerald had been outstanding throughout the entire playoffs and the Cardinals would likely have been nowhere near Tampa Bay for the Super Bowl if not for his superlative performance. He was also great in the regular season during the 2008 campaign with 96 catches for 1,431 yards and 12 touchdowns. However, he took it up a notch in the post-season when he scored a total of seven touchdowns while hauling in 30 catches for 546 yards. It was the best playoff performance by a wide receiver in NFL history — even better than the great Jerry Rice of the San Francisco 49ers. In the NFC championship game against the Philadelphia Eagles, Fitzgerald caught three TD passes and then made two important receptions as the Cardinals went down the field for the winning points to defeat the stubborn Eagles 32–25. It was as though the wideout had almost singlehandedly decided the Cardinals were not going to lose the title game. He also scored majors against Atlanta and Carolina to help the Cardinals reach the NFC championship game for the first time since they moved to the Arizona desert. The victory gave the Cardinals a shot at winning their first NFL title since 1947, when the team was located in Chicago.

IN THE HUDDLE

Fitzgerald set the Cardinals single-season franchise record with 103 receptions in 2005, the same year he led the league in receptions.

Fitzgerald was exposed to football at an early age and because his father, Larry Sr., was a Minneapolis football writer, he was able to become the ball boy for the Minnesota Vikings. He admired Vikings receiver Cris Carter and attended the NFC championship game when Minnesota got there in 1998 and lost 30–27 in overtime to Atlanta. He then attended the University of Pittsburgh before the Cardinals drafted him third overall in the 2004 NFL draft. The

6-foot-3, 220-pound Fitzgerald caught 58 passes as a rookie and then hauled in 103 in his second NFL campaign for 1,409 yards. He had a down year in 2006, but bounced back in 2007 to record another 1,409 receiving yards. Arizona was only 9–7 during the 2008 season despite a great year by Fitzgerald and two other 1,000-yard receivers in Anquan Boldin and Steve Breaston. Fitzgerald, having posted 1,400 or more yards in three of his five NFL seasons is now considered the best receiver in football.

The Cardinals recognized Fitzgerald's Pro Bowl status by signing him to a $40-million contact, the best deal given to a wide receiver in the entire league. Fitzgerald achieved his status by good old-fashioned hard work and he makes sure any ball thrown in his direction belongs to him. His jumping ability is beautiful to watch and he thrives on double coverage; as long as the quarterback makes the throw remotely catchable, Fitzgerald and his soft hands will come down with it.

It will be interesting to see if the Cardinals can keep their offense together. If they do, the Arizona club may yet end its long championship drought, and there is no doubt Fitzgerald will lead the way.

ANTONIO GATES

Before the 2008 season began, it was very unclear if San Diego Chargers tight end Antonio Gates would be able to play. He had off-season surgery to repair a dislocated big toe and the recovery process was very slow. The Chargers contemplated putting him on the "unable to perform" list, which would knock him out of the lineup for at least six weeks.

Gates was worried San Diego fans would not see No. 85 playing like his usual self. And when you consider a player like the 6-foot-4, 260-pounder needs to plant his foot to make hard turns and cuts to be effective, everyone's concern was certainly understandable. Somehow, Gates worked himself into condition and did not miss a single game during the season, catching 60 passes for 704 yards and scoring eight touchdowns. He recorded his 50th career TD when he caught two passes for majors in a Chargers win over Tampa Bay. By the end of the season his career reception total was an even 400 and his yardage total was 5,066 — all accomplished in just 93 total games. His great play helped the Chargers stage a late rally to take a playoff spot and earned Gates a spot in the Pro Bowl as a reserve. As it turned out, all the pre-season concern was totally unnecessary.

IN THE HUDDLE
Gates set a NFL tight end record by catching 50 touchdowns in his first 92 games.

Gates' rise to prominence is quite remarkable considering he never played a down of football while attending university at Kent State. Gates was a top basketball player, but when he was informed there was not future for him in the NBA, he started considering the advice many people had given him about trying football. The Chargers thought they saw something special in the young man and were one of many teams to express interest in Gates. San Diego GM A.J. Smith was able to secure the undrafted free agent to a deal and Gates began his NFL career in 2003. He joined a team that featured LaDainian Tomlinson at running back and Drew Brees at quarterback and the addition of Gates added significantly to their attack. Gates began slowly, but by the third month of the 2003 season, he was a starter and concluded the year with 24 catches for 389 yards and two touchdowns. With many teams intent on stopping

Tomlinson, Gates was able to take advantage of his size, speed and strength to get open for Brees. The pair connected for 81 completions, good for 964 yards and 13 TDs in 2004. Gates was now attracting plenty of attention, as were the Chargers, who made the playoffs.

The 2005 season was even better for Gates as he caught 89 balls for 1,101 yards and ten touchdowns despite missing one game due to a contract dispute. Gates was now a Pro Bowl player and a wealthy man with a six-year, $24-million deal in his pocket. The Chargers made a change at quarterback for the 2006 campaign, but installing Philip Rivers at the position was not any hindrance to Gates, who caught 71 passes for 924 yards and nine touchdowns. A loss to the New England Patriots in the playoffs kept the 14–2 Chargers from making a Super Bowl appearance.

As the 2007 season began, Gates was considered the premier tight end in football, slightly ahead of Kansas City's Tony Gonzalez. He had another outstanding season with 75 catches for 984 yards and nine touchdowns but, his post-season was marred by his toe injury and the banged-up Chargers lost to the Patriots in the AFC championship game. The 2008 season was lackluster for the Chargers as they squeaked into the post-season by winning their last four games on the schedule, narrowly taking the AFC West crown over the Denver Broncos. The playoffs started well for the Chargers as they dispatched the Indianapolis Colts with a 23–17 win, but they ultimately fell to the eventual Super Bowl champion Pittsburgh Steelers the next week, 35–24.

Gates is a gritty performer who can catch and block as well as any tight end in NFL history. If he can stay healthy, Gates has all the skills and abilities required to keep adding to his impressive numbers and earn a reputation as one of the best ever at his position.

CAREER HIGHLIGHTS

- Is the second-fastest player in league history to collect 5,000 yards receiving as a tight end.
- Five-time selection for the Pro Bowl (2004–2008).
- Signed with the Chargers as an undrafted free agent on May 2, 2003 out of Kent State University.
- In 2004 set the NFL single-season record for touchdown receptions by a tight end with 13.
- His 400 career receptions rank him third in league history among tight ends behind Tony Gonzalez of Atlanta and Jason Witten of Dallas.

TONY GONZALEZ

Big No. 88 for the Kansas City Chiefs was still performing like a youngster in 2008, despite hitting a relatively old football age of 32. Tony Gonzalez just keeps rolling along no matter who is at quarterback or where he is playing.

Because the Chiefs entered 2008 with the youngest average age of any team in the league (24.8) and 15 rookies on the 53-man roster, they were expected to struggle. Predictably, the team finished 2–14, tied for the NFL's second-worst record with the St. Louis Rams. Only 0–16 Detroit was looking up at Kansas City.

If the Chiefs' plans to go with a youthful lineup bothered Gonzalez, he in no way showed it and kept doing the things that made him a 10-time Pro Bowl player. He caught 96 passes for 1,058 yards and 10 touchdowns, a performance that only enhances Gonzalez's chances of making it to the Pro Football Hall of Fame one day.

In his 12 seasons with the Chiefs, Gonzalez only played in three playoff games, losing each one. Those post-season numbers are the only thing casting a shadow on the career of the best tight end in league history. From 1997 to 2008, the 6-foot-5, 251-pound Gonzalez has caught a total of 916 passes for 10,940 yards and 76 touchdowns. The only tight end in NFL annals whose numbers rival those totals is Shannon Sharpe.

Gonzalez has recorded 26 games in which he racked up 100 or more yards on pass receptions, an NFL record for tight ends. But the burly Gonzalez is about much more than numbers and was appreciated by former Kansas City coach Herm Edwards for being a consummate professional and leader on the field. Edwards also liked the fact he led by example rather than simply being someone who talked a lot in the locker room.

Gonzalez is also quick to credit his teammates for his success and singled out quarterback Tyler Thigpen — a virtual unknown before the season began — for helping his performance in 2008. He also does the necessary blocking required of anybody playing the tight end position.

IN THE HUDDLE

Gonzalez is the only tight end in league history to register six 100-yard receiving games in a single season, which he accomplished twice: 2000 and 2004.

Gonzalez made his annual trip to Hawaii to play in the Pro Bowl, where he was named the AFC starting tight end for the 2009 contest. The game is not much more than an exhibition contest, but he loves going and has taken his 90-year-old grandmother to the event for 10 straight years. As if he does not have enough records already, Gonzalez now holds the Pro Bowl mark for most career catches (39) in the all-star game, breaking Jerry Rice's mark of 37. He also topped Rice's old Pro Bowl mark for most career yards (495) by making

CAREER HIGHLIGHTS

• Ten-time Pro Bowl selection (1999–2008).

• Led the league in receptions with 102 in 2004.

• Holds Chiefs records in every major receiving category.

• Has racked up more consecutive 70-catch seasons (six), 60-catch seasons (ten) and 50-catch seasons (11) than any other tight end in NFL history.

six catches for 84 yards to bring his reception total to 590. Gonzalez caught one of his eight passes from Peyton Manning for a touchdown, tying him with Jimmy Smith and Marvin Harrison for the all-time Pro Bowl record with five majors scored.

Given the Chief's rebuilding state, former Kansas City president Carl Peterson toyed with the idea of trading Gonzalez — with the player's approval — at the trade deadline, but did not pull the trigger. The lack of a deal caused a strain between Peterson — who resigned after 20 years in charge of the Chiefs — and Gonzalez, but the always-reliable player went back out and played as hard as ever. Despite being competitive in many of its losses, Kansas City had a hugely disappointing year that

ultimately cost coach Edwards his job when Scott Pioli was put in charge of the Chiefs' operations.

Pioli named Todd Haley as the new head coach, and it was determined that in the best interest of the Kansas club that Gonzalez be moved if the right offer came along. The Atlanta Falcons decided that the future Hall of Famer would be another good target for quarterback Matt Ryan, and nabbed Gonzalez for a second round draft choice in 2010. Everyone associated with the Chiefs was sad to see Gonzalez leave, but it could be very exciting to see what he adds to the Falcons attack in the short term. At most Gonzalez will play a couple more seasons, and it is his hope that Atlanta delivers the final piece of his career puzzle — a Super Bowl.

PITTSBURGH STEELERS
★ ★ ★
WIDE RECEIVER
10

SANTONIO HOLMES

With the final minute of Super Bowl XLIII underway, the Pittsburgh Steelers were driving for the winning score. Everyone expected quarterback Ben Roethlisberger to look for Hines Ward or perhaps Heath Miller as they lined up at the Arizona six-yard line, down 23–20 to the Cardinals. But when Roethlisberger could not find anyone open, he spotted Santonio Holmes in the back corner of the end zone and heaved a high toss to the 5-foot-11 wide receiver. Holmes was the only person with a shot at making the catch, despite the fact three Cardinal defensive backs were all in the area. In order to do it, Holmes stretched every inch of his body to take the ball in both hands while making sure his feet

were both down in the end zone. He crashed to the turf, but cradled the ball throughout and after a few minutes of official review, the call stood — touchdown! The Steelers had the lead with only 35 seconds to play and hung on for a 27–23 victory.

IN THE HUDDLE
Holmes ranked first in the NFL in 2007 with 18.1 yards per reception.

The fact Holmes was able to pull off such a spectacular play should come as no surprise to anyone who followed the 2008 NFL playoffs. The Steelers first faced the San Diego Chargers

and won the contest 35–24 with Holmes returning a punt 67 yards for a touchdown. Then in the AFC championship game, he and Roethlisberger improvised to complete a 65-yard pass-and-run play to give the Steelers a 13–0 lead over the Baltimore Ravens en route to a 23–14 victory. Holmes was also no slouch during the regular season when he took in a career-high 55 catches for 821 yards and five touchdowns. He added four more major scores in the post-season, but saved his best performance for the Super Bowl when he caught nine passes — including the game-winner — for a total of 131 yards. He was at his best during the Steelers' final drive and his 40-yard pass-and-run reception got Pittsburgh in position to win the game. Holmes was named MVP of the game and soon everyone was talking about the player who was going to Disney World the next day.

To say Holmes came from humble beginnings would be quite an understatement. He was born in Belle Glade, Florida, one of the poorest rural areas of the country. He hunted rabbits when he was seven and eight years old (with out a gun) just to make extra money. He would get between $3 and $5 for each hare, but as he got older, Holmes turned to selling drugs on street corners, even though he claims he never used them himself.

Making money as a dealer was easy, but he soon came to realize it was no way to live because he certainly didn't want to end up in jail. Holmes' mother moved the youth away from the crime element, and the transition allowed the youngster to concentrate on sports — and he loved football. He had starred on very good teams in high school, earning two Florida state titles along the way to attending Ohio State University. He was the Steelers' first round draft pick in 2006 at 25th overall and has been on an upward trajectory since landing in Pittsburgh. Holmes has increased his pass-reception total every year, recording 49 his first season and following that up with 52 in 2007 before his best year in 2008.

Holmes made it a point to talk about where and how he grew up during the week of the Super Bowl so that if any youngster was in the same position as he was, they might be inspired by his story. It is interesting to note Holmes was benched for one game in the 2008 regular season because he was charged with drug possession. The 189-pound receiver claims the drugs police found in his car were not his and that they belonged to someone else who was driving his vehicle. If Holmes is indeed reformed, he will likely use his Super Bowl fame for all the right causes. His spectacular catch to win the championship game will go down as one of the sport's greatest moments. It would be a shame if fans didn't hold the man who made the play in the same high regard.

CAREER HIGHLIGHTS

- Named Super Bowl XLIII MVP finishing with nine catches for 131 yards and a game-winning touchdown.
- Named NFL rookie of the week following Week 6 of the 2006 season.
- Second cousin of Jacksonville Jaguars All-Pro running back Fred Taylor.

SEATTLE SEAHAWKS
★ ★ ★
WIDE RECEIVER
84

T.J. HOUSHMANDZADEH

When January 2009 flipped to February and free agency day loomed, the Cincinnati Bengals had yet to reach out to receiver T.J. Houshmandzadeh.

Coming off a season where the Bengals were 4–11–1, Houshmandzadeh (hoosh-man-ZAH-deh) still found a way to rank sixth in the NFL with 92 receptions, one season after his 112 catches tied New England's Wes Welker for the league lead. In 2007, his work came as the Bengals put up a record of 7–9.

Since his Cincinnati arrival in 2001, Houshmandzadeh put up 507 receptions for 5,782 yards and 37 touchdowns through his first eight NFL seasons — one of which (2003) was limited to two games because of a nagging hamstring.

When a deal wasn't worked out with Cincinnati, Houshmandzadeh took to the airwaves and interview circuit, letting several NFL squads know he'd be more than happy to settle wherever the best offer presented itself. As it turned out, the Seattle Seahawks landed the

off-season's best free agent receiver, inking him to what was believed to be a five-year, $40-million pact.

This receiver known for hanging on to virtually anything thrown his way will keep making the catches in Seattle that elevated him to elite status during his time in Cincinnati.

IN THE HUDDLE

Houshmandzadeh scored at least one TD in the first eight games of the 2007 season, the longest single-season, consecutive-games touchdown streak in Bengals history.

The troubled Bengals began the season with eight consecutive losses and were 1–11–1 before winning their final three games of the season. Cincinnati tied the Cleveland Browns and the St. Louis Rams for a league-low 20 touchdowns in 2008, each with 11 through the air and six rushing. Quarterback Ryan Fitzpatrick tossed eight TD passes and Carson Palmer three, with Chad Ochocinco matching Houshmandzadeh for a team-high four touchdown receptions.

Houshmandzadeh's most productive campaign came in 2007, when his 112 catches netted 1,143 yards and 12 touchdowns. He paced Cincinnati receivers in catches from 2006 through 2008 and his 904 receiving yards in 2008 made him

the Bengals' leader in that category for the first time in his career. Next to Ochocinco (612) and Carl Perkins (530), Houshmandzadeh's 507 receptions through 2008 placed him third on the Bengals' all-time list.

Touraj Houshmandzadeh was born to an African-American mother and Iranian father on September 26, 1977 in the San Bernardino, California, county of Victor Valley. His hometown is Barstow, among the cities that comprise Victor Valley.

While in his senior year at Barstow High School, Houshmandzadeh was a standout running back for a team that went 10–1–1. He then moved on to Cerritos College, where he converted to wide receiver. He took off in that role, while also spending some time as a kick returner, where he twice carried kickoffs back for 100 yards and a punt for almost 90 yards.

Oregon State came calling and Houshmandzadeh accepted the scholarship opportunity. The move

also allowed him to hook up with Chad Johnson — who has legally changed his name to Chad Ochocinco — for the first time. Houshmandzadeh turned in a solid senior year for the No. 4-ranked Beavers with 48 receptions for 730 yards and seven TDs. Ochocinco added 37 catches for 806 yards and eight TDs, including two in the Fiesta Bowl win over Notre Dame. The Bengals ended up drafting both Beavers — Ochocinco in the second round at No. 36 overall and Houshmandzadeh way down in the seventh round at 204th.

Houshmandzadeh's early NFL years were affected by injuries. But when Peter Warrick was sidelined in 2004, a chance to redefine his role with the Bengals presented itself.

Houshmandzadeh caught passes in the final 10 contests of that season and in the first 12 of 2005. That 22-game streak stands as a Bengals record. And the Oregon State duo of

CAREER HIGHLIGHTS

- Led the NFL with 112 receptions in 2007.
- Is third place on the Bengals' all-time receptions list with 507.
- Selected to Pro Bowl in 2007.
- Is fifth in Bengals history with 37 touchdown receptions.

Houshmandzadeh, wearing jersey No. 84, and Ochocinco, with No. 85, became a dynamic duo.

By the time Houshmandzadeh's contract expired with the Bengals following 2008, there was no more confusion as to how his last name is pronounced. A commercial for fantasy football once had a would-be participant call him "Who's Your Momma," a phrase Ochocinco also came to use in reference to his former teammate. Houshmandzadeh is now a known quantity and no longer underrated.

HOUSTON TEXANS
★ ★ ★
WIDE RECEIVER
80

ANDRE JOHNSON

Andre Lamont Johnson of the Houston Texans made it to the Pro Football Hall of Fame in 2008 despite being only 27 years old.

Check that, Johnson's jersey and gloves along with the ball he caught following his record-setting performance in Week 17 against Chicago have a permanent spot in Canton, Ohio; Johnson will have to wait quite a while to see if he'll make a similar trip.

It was his 10 catches (for 148 yards and two TDs) versus the Bears that were of significance in 2008, as Johnson became the first NFLer with seven games of 10-or-more catches in one season. The Texans were a stellar 6–1 in those contests.

Johnson also equaled two other NFL records in 2008. He went three consecutive games with 10-or-more catches — 10 for 178 yards versus Miami in Week 6; 11 for 141 yards versus Detroit in Week 7 and 11 for 143 yards against Cincinnati in Week 8 — and four games in a row with 130-or-more yards, starting with 131 yards on nine receptions against Indianapolis in Week 5.

Facing the potent Tennessee Titans during Week 15, Johnson snared 11 passes for 207 yards and one TD in the 13–12 triumph. He became one of three players in 2008 — and the first Texan ever — to reach 200 yards receiving in one game, joining Terrell Owens of the Dallas Cowboys and Antonio Bryant of the Tampa Bay Buccaneers.

Johnson led Houston in receiving in each of his first six years with the club, but none of his totals compared to his work in 2008 when he led the league and set franchise highs with 1,575 yards and 115 receptions. He also paced the NFL in pass receptions with 103 in 2006.

Quarterbacks Matt Schaub

CAREER HIGHLIGHTS

- Led the NFL in receiving yards per game in 2007 with 94.6 yards.
- Three time Pro Bowl selection (2004, 2006, 2008).
- Led all AFC rookies in receptions and receiving yards in 2003.
- First player in 2008 to reach 100 receptions when he accomplished the feat on December 21 in Oakland.

and Sage Rosenfels took full advantage of Johnson's skill, once again bringing the Texans on the brink of their first post-season appearance. They fell short in that quest, but a first-time appearance by Houston on *Monday Night Football* was another indication the Texans are finally a team to watch.

The Texans hit the NFL scene in 2002 and lived through five losing seasons before breaking even at 8–8 in 2007 and again in 2008. Johnson is a shining example of their approach to build through the draft. Leaving the Miami Hurricanes following his junior year, Johnson was the second wide receiver taken in the 2003 draft and the third player taken overall. He was, however, the first pass-catcher out of that draft class to live up to his billing, as Charles Rogers of the Detroit Lions — the No. 2 pick — was a bust.

IN THE HUDDLE
Johnson has twice led the NFL in receptions: 2006 with 103 and 2008 with 115.

Johnson's tenure with the Hurricanes included the 2001 national title, the school's first crown in a decade. The Hurricanes put the finishing exclamation point on their 12–0 season with a 37–14 win over No. 4-ranked Nebraska in the Rose Bowl. Canes quarterback Ken Dorsey and Johnson shared the MVP award in the championship game — which illustrated just how good Johnson was, considering the squad also included the likes of running back Clinton Portis, tight end Jeremy Shockey and free safety Ed Reed.

Since 2003, Johnson — or "Dre" as his teammates call him — has been splendid in the NFL. He is extremely quick

for a man who's 6-foot-3 and weighs 223 pounds. Despite the relatively mild attention paid to the Texans over the years, his achievements haven't been overlooked considering his All-Pro selections in 2006 and 2008 along with his Pro Bowl trips in 2004, 2006 and 2008.

The Miami native also spent part of his formative years on the Gulf side of the Sunshine State in Clearwater before returning to his birthplace. A wide receiver of renown at Miami Senior High School, Johnson also lettered

in basketball and track and field. At college, he sparked the Hurricanes on the gridiron and on the track, where he dashed to Big East titles indoors over 60-meters and outdoors in the 100-meter sprint.

The finish line for him now is to see the Texans forge the same winning mark he helped create at every level of his sporting pursuits. If he keeps producing the way he has thus far, one day he may carve out his own spot in the Hall of Fame.

DETROIT LIONS
★ ★ ★

WIDE RECEIVER
81

CALVIN JOHNSON

CAREER HIGHLIGHTS

- Led all rookies in 2007 with 15.8 yards per reception.
- Named a Pro Bowl alternate for 2008.
- Was fifth in receiving yards in 2008 with 1,331.
- Over his first two years Johnson has appeared in 31 of a possible 32 games.

How good was wide receiver Calvin Johnson for the 0–16 Detroit Lions in 2008? Awesome enough to merit an "A" grading in an "F"-marked report card issued by the *Detroit Free Press* at the merciful end of the woeful season and give long-suffering Lions Nation something, *anything* to cheer about for the upcoming 2009 campaign. He also provides some hope that after a bad run of drafting poor receivers with high picks, the Lions may have finally found their man.

In the years leading up to Johnson's selection, the Lions drafted three other receivers: Charles Rogers in 2003, Roy Williams in 2004 and Mike Williams in 2005. Rogers and Mike Williams ended up spending very little time in the NFL while Roy Willams was dealt to Dallas.

Johnson was taken No. 2 overall in 2007 and so far, things are really panning out.

As a rookie signed to a six-year contract in 2007, Johnson started 10 of the 15 games he played, making 48 catches for 756 yards and four touchdowns. He even rushed four times for 52 yards and a touchdown. But as a sophomore, Johnson lived up to the billing of his "Spider-Man" nickname, making like the Marvel Comics superhero to use his 6-foot-5, 239-pound frame to cling to 78 catches for 1,331 yards and tying Arizona's Larry Fitzgerald for the league lead with 12 TDs.

Herman Moore, in 1995, was the first Lion with at least 70 catches, 1,200 yards and 10 touchdowns in a season and Johnson can boast that he is the second. Johnson doesn't lack confidence and believes his hands are even better Fitzgerald's. Johnson would love to see the Lions stage a turnaround like the Cardinals provided in 2008 where the perennial sad-sack squad almost defied logic and won the Super Bowl.

The Yellow Jackets, past and present, swelled with pride when Johnson became the ninth Georgia Tech footballer to go in the first round and highest-ever drafted from that school, besting running back Eddie Prokop who went No. 4 overall to the Boston Patriots way back in 1945.

Born in Tyrone, Georgia on September 25, 1985, Johnson drew a lot of attention from a young age because he put up such stunning numbers with a swift, sure-handed large frame. Georgia Tech was delighted to land him and Johnson didn't disappoint, leaving as perhaps the greatest wide receiver in school history. In his senior year, Johnson, whose career numbers with the Yellow Jackets included 28 TDs and 2,927 yards in receptions, captured the Fred Biletnikoff Award as the top collegiate receiver.

Aside from his playmaking on the field, Johnson scored heavily with an off-field project he undertook in 2006 when he decided to help the less fortunate. He had two options that summer: Help out with designs for environmentally friendly luxury condos less than a mile away from Georgia Tech or design and build solar latrines to improve sanitation in Bolivia.

For Johnson, it was, "Bolivia, here I come," and he was more than happy to participate in

a project that made a global difference.

However, a bit of a controversy involving Johnson erupted in 2007. At the pre-draft NFL combine that year, Johnson, Clemson defensive end Gaines Adams and Louisville defensive tackle Amobi Okoye admitted, in confidence, that they had used marijuana.

Word leaked out before the draft, but rather than be castigated, the trio openly admitted to their drug use and was heralded for their honesty. Each player ultimately got drafted in the first round.

Johnson even reinforced his stance on drug use, stating his marijuana use was a thing of the past from his younger days in college. The Lions were convinced of that and, despite queries for their No. 2 pick, they held on and pounced on Johnson after Oakland opted for LSU quarterback JaMarcus Russell at No. 1.

Johnson's achievements as a sophomore in the NFL were noteworthy considering the Lions' record and the revolving door at quarterback. During 2008, his seven catches of 40-plus yards (including one TD catch-and-run play of 96 yards) and 21 receptions of 20-plus yards each tied for second-most in the NFL.

The Lions might have been lousy in 2008, but Calvin Johnson was terrific.

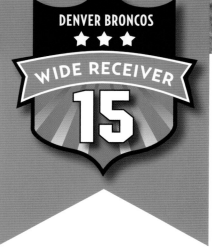

DENVER BRONCOS
★ ★ ★
WIDE RECEIVER
15

BRANDON MARSHALL

To say Denver Broncos wide receiver Brandon Marshall had a troubled off-season prior to the start of the 2008 NFL campaign might be the understatement of the year. A domestic dispute and a terrible at-home accident that injured his arm were just two issues Marshall had to bounce back from before the start of the new season. He also had encounters with the police (three times in total over the previous 12 months) and a talk with NFL commissioner Roger Goodell before he was allowed to return. His indiscretions landed him a three-game suspension from the league, which was later reduced to one game and two games' pay. Add to that the commentary of former Broncos quarterback Jay Cutler, who said his talented teammate was simply too immature. However, Marshall was determined to put it all behind him and wanted to prove he was much wiser by learning from his mistakes.

In his first game of the 2008 season Marshall made 18 catches against the San Diego Chargers for 166 yards and a touchdown in the Broncos' 39–38 victory. His 18 receptions set a new team record and were just short of the NFL record held by Terrell Owens, who once caught 20 in a game. He also had 11 catches against Kansas City and 10 against Buffalo in late-season contests to give him a total of 104 receptions — the third-best mark in the league — for 1,265 yards during the 2008 season. His performance landed Marshall a spot on the AFC starting team for the end-of-season Pro Bowl. Being named to the prestigious team was a vindication of sorts for Marshall, but he must stay out of trouble.

Marshall's performance in 2008 should actually not come as much of a surprise. He was also outstanding in 2007, when he caught 102 balls for 1,325 yards, giving him an average of 13.0 yards per reception. Marshall had missed most of training

IN THE HUDDLE
Led the NFL in receiving yards after contact in 2007, totalling 319 yards following initial contact with a defender.

camp with injuries prior to the start of the 2007 season and the thinking was he would not be ready to start the year. But he did not miss a game and showed a talent for the wide receiver position that was not always previously evident. In fact, many people wondered if he might be better suited as a tight end. At 6-foot-4 and 230 pounds, Marshall is very physically imposing and does not play a finesse sort of game. He would much rather run defensive backs over than try to avoid them, and more than one opponent has said Marshall might be the hardest receiver to bring down in a one-on-one situation. When Javon Walker left the Broncos, Marshall was in great position to take over as the

team's primary target. Denver also boasts three other quality pass-catchers in Tony Scheffler, Brandon Stokley and Eddie Royal.

The Broncos drafted Marshall 119th overall in 2006 after he had attended the University of Central Florida. In 44 college games he made 112 receptions for 1,674 yards and 13 touchdowns. He was named MVP of the 2005 Hawaii Bowl when he had 11 catches for 210 yards and scored three TDs in the game — his best performance in college. He suffered a ligament injury after being drafted by Denver, but still managed to play in 15 games as a rookie. He made 20 receptions in the 2006 season, finishing the year strongly by making a catch in each of his last seven games; Marshall took one of those receptions all the way for a 71-yard score. His performance at the end of 2006 certainly gave Marshall the confidence he needed to become a full-time performer in 2007 and a star in 2008.

Denver has a new offense-minded coach in Josh McDaniels and he will be counting on Marshall to keep up his great performance, especially given that star quarterback Cutler was traded to Chicago in the off-season. Marshall used his time at the Pro Bowl to observe, and if being around great players is a good influence on him, he should be able to fulfill his enormous potential.

CAREER HIGHLIGHTS

- Had three 10-catch games for the Broncos in 2007 and became the first player in team history to record consecutive outings with at least 10 receptions.
- Drafted 119th overall from the University of Central Florida by the Denver Broncos in 2006.
- Selected to the Pro Bowl in 2008.
- Became the second player in Broncos history to have consecutive 100-catch seasons (Rod Smith in 2000–01).

RANDY MOSS

Randy Moss entered the NFL in 1998 with the Minnesota Vikings, and almost instantly became a star with his loud style both on and off the field. But, by 2006, his second season with the Oakland Raiders, the wide receiver posted his worst performance in his career. Moss had made just 42 catches for 563 yards and only three touchdowns that year. More than one observer thought Moss was too slow and had simply lost his desire to be a standout player. Enter the Super Bowl-champion New England Patriots, who thought the 6-foot-4, 210-pound receiver still had something to offer and completed a trade with Oakland prior to the start of the 2007 season. The Pats believed their winning environment would persuade Moss to use his immense talent for good instead of looking for more trouble. To the surprise of everyone except New England management, the plan worked — almost to perfection.

As soon as he became a Patriot, Moss realized he was on a special team and had a key role to play. It also helped that he had a great quarterback in Tom Brady throwing him the ball. They connected on 98 passes, good for 1,493 yards, and 23 touchdowns through the air — an NFL record. Moss missed most of training camp prior to the start of 2007, but was ready to go in the opener when he caught nine passes for 183 yards and one TD on a 51-yard toss from Brady in a 38–14 win over the New York Jets. New England rolled through the season with an undefeated 16–0 mark, defeating the other New York team, the Giants, 38–35 on the last night of the regular campaign. In that game, Moss scored two majors, the second one breaking the record for the most TDs caught in one season held by former San Francisco 49er great Jerry Rice. Moss was

CAREER HIGHLIGHTS

- Six-time Pro Bowl selection (1998–2000, 2002, 2003, 2007).
- 1998 Associated Press offensive rookie of the year.
- Led the NFL in receiving touchdowns four times (1998, 2000, 2003, 2007).
- Set an NFL record for the most receiving yards in a player's first seven seasons. His 9,142 yards topped Jerry Rice's 9,072.

named the AFC player of the week two times, while Brady won the same recognition five times for the utterly dominating Patriots. The Giants, however, extracted their revenge and ended New England's chances of running the table with a 17–14 Super Bowl win. Moss scored one touchdown in the loss. Over the course of 2007, Moss showed that any concern about how he would fit in to the Patriots team was totally unfounded.

IN THE HUDDLE
Moss set a rookie record for most touchdowns in a season with 17 receiving TDs.

Most thought Moss would be a very high selection in his 1998 draft year, but he wasn't taken until Minnesota nabbed him at No. 21 overall. Many teams — including those who needed help at wide receiver — passed on Moss due to his off-field behavior. His problems started before he even went to college. Notre Dame was set to welcome Moss, but his involvement in a racial riot at his high school forced the Fighting Irish to release him before he even arrived. He ultimately pled guilty to battery charges stemming from the riot. He then tried to get into Florida State, but a drug issue while he was on parole for the battery sentence scuttled that notion.

He ended up staring at Marshall University, a Division II school that won a national championship with an undefeated record. Moss vowed to make teams regret passing on him in the draft. He was spectacular in his NFL rookie campaign — hauling in 69 catches for 1,313 yards, 17 touchdowns and averaging a whopping 19.0 yards per catch.

His great hands were obvious, but it was his ability to make tacklers miss that truly stood out. He didn't miss a game in his first six seasons and was over 1,200 receiving yards each year, with a career-best 1,632 yards in 2003. The Vikings never made it to the Super Bowl, but had a great year in Moss' rookie season when they went 15–1 before losing to Atlanta in the NFC title game.

The seasons between 2004 and 2006 were essentially lost years for Moss and included a trade from Minnesota to Oakland. The Vikings simply had their fill of Moss' antics and the Raiders were also quick to criticize him when they felt he was out of line. Moss seemed to take the harsh assessment by Oakland in stride and saw a new beginning with the Patriots. When Brady went down with a season-ending injury in 2008, Moss became a team leader and did his best to help Matt Cassel make a difficult transition to the role of starting QB. His teammates saw a player dedicated to winning and even named him one of the team captains. Not many people would have imagined that just a few years ago.

STEVE SMITH

Competitive fire has made the Carolina Panthers' Steve Smith one of the most elite wide receivers in the NFL since 2001, but it has also gotten him into trouble. After battling his anger in the past, his management of that emotion escaped him once more in August of 2008. That's when he broke the nose of teammate and cornerback Ken Lucas during a sideline dispute at training camp.

The Panthers immediately sent their star receiver home and suspended him for the first two games of 2008. Smith apologized for the incident. To their credit, rather than let the whole situation tear them apart, everyone, including Smith, pulled together like a strong family getting over internal bickering.

Carolina won the NFC South title with a 12–4 record and had the second seed in the NFC behind the New York Giants. Smith's production was affected by his suspension, particularly with the number of receptions he made — 78 compared to 87 in 2007, 83 in 2006 and a career-best/franchise-record 103 in 2005. But Smith was third in receiving yards in 2008 with 1,421, the second-highest total of his NFL career aside from his franchise-record 1,563 in 2005.

IN THE HUDDLE
Smith captured the NFL's "Triple Crown" leading all receivers in 2005 in receiving yards (1,563), receptions (103) and receiving touchdowns (12).

No one could catch Smith in 2008 in terms of 20-plus yard receptions; he had 23, two more than Green Bay's Greg Jennings and Detroit's Calvin Johnson. He also led the league in average receiving yards per game — 101.5 compared to 98.4 by Houston's Andre Johnson — and yards averaged per catch (18.2) for all players with 70-or-more receptions.

The All-Pro selectors gave Andre Johnson and Arizona's Larry Fitzgerald the top two spots in the 2008 voting at 45 and 21 votes, respectively. But Smith was the only other wide receiver to merit double

figures in votes with 16.

At 5-foot-9 and 185 pounds, Smith always had to prove his worth along the way. He was drafted in 2001 out of Utah in the third round (74th overall). Smith became the only rookie to earn a trip to the Pro Bowl after the 2001 season as the result of his spectacular kick returning. He was the only player that year to return a kick and a punt for TDs.

He started once as a rookie, but won the chance to start as a wide receiver out of training camp in 2002. The high of being a factor in Carolina's close loss to New England in Super Bowl XXXVIII was euphoric. But at the opposite end of the picture, his dreams for 2004 were shattered in the season opener against Green Bay. On the sixth catch he made for his 60th yard, he broke his left fibula on the tackle and spent the entire season on the sidelines.

Undaunted, he returned in 2005 to tie Fitzgerald for the NFL lead in receptions (103) and pace the league in reception yards (1,563). That season, Smith shared the Associated Press comeback player of the year award with New England linebacker Tedy Bruschi.

Encountering and overcoming challenges has defined the native of Lynwood, which is located in Los Angeles County, California. Raised in a single-parent home, Smith's mother, Florence Young, was involved in drug counseling. His exposure to her workplace made Smith promise to stay away from drugs. He took the bus to his job at a fast-food restaurant and his visits back home to Los Angeles now still include re-connecting with his childhood roots.

At L.A.'s University High School, Smith starred in football as well as track and field. He then attended Santa Monica College for two years, a school blessed to have him and another future NFL receiver, Chad Johnson. Transferring to the University of Utah, Smith continued to build his credentials as a kick returner/wide receiver.

Smith has twice made the All-Pro Team (2001 and 2005) and has been a Pro Bowler on four occasions

CAREER HIGHLIGHTS

- Awarded the 2005 comeback player of the year.
- Four-time Pro Bowl selection (2001, 2005, 2006, 2008)
- In 2002 Smith became the second player in NFL history to return two punts for touchdowns in the same game that he recorded a reception for a touchdown.

(2001, 2005, 2006 and 2008). Extremely community minded, he's a solid family man and much of his enjoyment for trips to the Pro Bowl in Honolulu came from spending time there with his wife and three children.

In preparing for life after football, Smith has taken time to study and intern in financial planning. Turning 30 in 2009, Smith still has much left for football. He proved that once more in 2008, a season that could have been derailed even before it started.

PITTSBURGH STEELERS
★ ★ ★
WIDE RECEIVER
86

HINES WARD

To put it simply, wide receiver Hines Ward does it all for the Pittsburgh Steelers. He not only catches any ball thrown in his direction, Ward also blocks fearlessly and sticks his nose in any scrum where the Pittsburgh needs to be represented. If there is a tackle to be made because of an interception, you can bet Ward will be hustling all over the field to bring the man down. Given his approach to the game, it was a wonder why so many people thought Ward would miss Super Bowl XLIII just because he had a sprained ligament in his knee.

With two weeks to prepare,

Ward worked feverishly around the clock to get ready. A doctor drew blood from the receiver, removing cells and concentrating them for use in an injection to the injured area. This was considered an unconventional and untested treatment for this type of injury, but Ward was willing to try anything that would help him play. It worked for a short time as Ward helped the Steelers score on the opening drive, but his final stats show only two catches on the day for 43 yards.

He later admitted his knee sprain got worse as the game wore on, but he never let on that he was

having trouble and stayed in the contest. He might not have been his usual self, but the Arizona Cardinals had to account for Ward's presence and that might have given fellow wide receiver Santonio Holmes a little more room to operate — perhaps leading to Holmes' choice as the MVP of the contest for his game-winning catch.

Ward has known much adversity in his life, which began in Seoul, South Korea, on March 8, 1976. His African-American father, Hines Sr., was a serviceman there when he met Ward's mother Kim, a Korean native. The family moved to the United States just after he turned one, but the marriage fell apart. Hines Sr. re-married and took Hines with him to Louisiana, but left the youngster with his grandmother. Sympathetic to Hines' mother, Ward's grandmother eventually returned him back to Kim. The 10-year-old Ward had little appreciation for how hard his mother's life was, being a single parent in a foreign country with little understanding of the language. He was sent back to his father, who made him understand in no uncertain terms that he had to respect his mom's situation. Ward came to see just how hard his mother worked to give him the best life she could. Ward stayed out of trouble and completed his homework every day while becoming a very good

athlete in high school playing both football and baseball. He also became more comfortable with his mixed heritage, no easy task for a somewhat confused and angry teenager.

IN THE HUDDLE
Ward is the Steelers' all-time leader in receptions (800), receiving yards (9,780) and receiving touchdowns (72).

Ward was heavily recruited and chose to attend Georgia, where he played quarterback, tailback and receiver for the Bulldogs. It took a while, but by 1997 he was the best player on the team and hauled in 55 passes despite the fact other teams were keying on him. The Steelers drafted the 6-foot, 215-pound Ward with the 92nd pick of the 1998 draft. Many thought Ward would never play in the NFL, but he soon proved his doubters wrong.

Pittsburgh obviously had some hesitancy as well because it took wide receivers with higher draft picks prior to selecting Ward. However, it was Ward who proved to be the best Steeler of them all once they found the right spot to play the talented receiver. For a while, Ward and Plaxico Burress were a great combination at the wide receiver position with each gaining over 1,000 yards in receptions in 2001. In 2002, Ward made a career-high 112 catches, but by 2003 the Steelers were very frustrated at not getting to the Super Bowl. Their record dropped to 6–10 in 2003, but they bounced back in 2004 under the guidance of rookie quarterback Ben Roethlisberger, making it all the way to the AFC championship game before bowing out to the New England Patriots.

Burress was allowed to leave before the 2005 season began, meaning Ward was now the star of the receiving corps. He was given a new contract worth $25.5 million and he responded by

CAREER HIGHLIGHTS
- Four-time Pro Bowl selection (2001–2004).
- Was named Steelers team MVP three times (2002, 2003, 2005).
- Was named Super Bowl XL MVP.

making 69 catches for 975 yards and 11 touchdowns. The Steelers finally made it to the Super Bowl in 2006 and beat the Seahawks 21–10 with Ward earning MVP honors by catching five passes for 123 yards and one TD reception. Soon afterwards he made a triumphant return to South Korea where he was treated like a conquering hero.

2006 and 2007 were not the best years by Pittsburgh's lofty standards, but 2008 proved magical once again. Ward made his 800th career reception during the season and recorded 1,043 receiving yards.

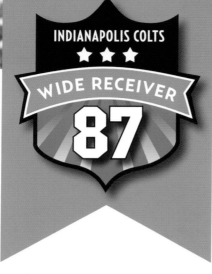

REGGIE WAYNE

CAREER HIGHLIGHTS

- His 53 career TD receptions rank him third in Indianapolis Colts history.
- Three-time Pro Bowl selection (2006–2008).
- Five consecutive seasons compiling at least 1,000 yards receiving (2004–2008).
- Has started 97 consecutive games to lead all NFL receivers.

Reggie Wayne's third consecutive trip to Aloha Stadium for the 2009 Pro Bowl felt very much like a college reunion. During his time with the Miami Hurricanes from 1997–2000, the gifted Indianapolis Colts wide receiver played with a significant number of players who eventually became impact players at the pro level.

In the 30th — and for now, final — edition of the Pro Bowl in Honolulu, the Hurricanes boasted more representatives than any other collegiate program. They included Wayne's old college roommate, Baltimore free safety Ed Reed; wide receiver Andre Thornton (Houston Texans); running back Clinton Portis (Washington Redskins); linebackers Ray Lewis (Baltimore) and Jon Beason (Carolina Panthers), and punter Jeff Feagles (New York Giants).

Wayne had just completed his eighth NFL season — and fifth in a row — where he surpassed the 1,000-yard mark in pass receptions. That should come as no surprise. With quarterback Peyton Manning at the controls and a receiving corps that has boasted wide receivers the likes of Marvin Harrison and Wayne along with tight end Dallas Clark, the Indianapolis passing attack has, for years, been something to behold.

Drafted in the first round's 30th position in 2001, Wayne began with 27 receptions for 345 yards as a rookie. He became the third player in NFL history to increase his reception total in each of his first seven seasons, posting 86 receptions for 1,310 yards in 2006 (his sixth season), and then besting himself in 2007 with 104 receptions, third-best in the NFL that season.

IN THE HUDDLE

In 2006 Wayne became the fifth player since the NFL/AFL merger (1970) to record a TD reception at the Super Bowl and the Pro Bowl in the same season.

It was a knee injury to Harrison that season that put the spotlight on Wayne more than it had ever been before. The 6-foot, 198-pounder confounded the double coverage he was facing and provided a number of spectacular catches in the process. His 1,510 receiving yards in 2007 ranked him first in the league. He dropped off to 82 receptions in 2008, but made sure he cleared 1,000 yards.

What Wayne has produced in the post-season further reinforces his own brand of greatness. After 13 playoff games in the first eight seasons of his career, he was the Colts' all-time post-season leader in receptions (66), receiving yards (963) and TDs (8). And next to kickers Adam Vinatieri (60 points) and Mike Vanderjagt (54 points), Wayne had the third-most playoff points in Colts history with 50.

Reginald Wayne was born in New Orleans, Louisiana, on November 17, 1978. He grew up in a middle-class community in that metropolitan area's West Bank and was a standout high school athlete in football and track and field with the John Ehret Patriots.

He's admitted New England was his original NFL team of choice based on a combination of his hometown New Orleans Saints perpetually struggling and his alma mater being nicknamed "Patriots." Of course, that all changed once he got into the Colts–Patriots rivalry. Wayne

was a big contributor to one of the biggest wins in Indianapolis history in the 2007 AFC championship game. The Colts were down 21–6 at the half, but came back to win a thriller by outscoring the Patriots 17–6 in the fourth quarter to squeak out a 38–34 victory. Wayne provided five catches for 68 yards, but two catches landed the Colts gains of 11 and 14 yards on the drive that put the Indianapolis ahead with 1:02 to go.

Two weeks later, Wayne scored his team's only receiving TD on a 53-yard play with Manning in Indy's 29–17 win over the Chicago Bears in Super Bowl XLI.

All the while, Wayne has constantly lived in the long shadow of Marvin Harrison, who after his 13th NFL season in 2008 — his last with the Colts as he was released in the off-season — was the record holder for the Colts in receptions

(1,102), receiving yards (14,508), touchdown receptions (128) and 100-plus yard games (59).

Wayne entered 2009 at No. 3 in Colts history (behind Harrison and Raymond Berry) in receptions (576), receiving yards (8,129) and TDs (53). Berry's career numbers of 631 catches for 9,275 yards and 68 TDs are milestones Wayne is set to pass. In terms of 100-plus yard games, Wayne is second to Harrison with 26.

As Wayne takes over the leading role in Indy, he will undoubtedly look back on his 2006 and 2007 seasons for strength, years in which his personal and team successes was accomplished with a heavy heart, as his brother, Rashad, died in September 2006 after losing control of his truck on a New Orleans highway. Yet, in spirit, Wayne believes his brother has been with him every step of the way.

NEW ENGLAND PATRIOTS ★ ★ ★
WIDE RECEIVER
83

WESS WELKER

Wes Welker doesn't believe in rejection. He's faced a lot of it throughout his football life, but he persevered until he got what he wanted.

Welker hails from Oklahoma City, Oklahoma, where his parents, Leland and Shelley, and older brother, Lee, have always believed he could etch out a career in pro football. Born on May 1, 1981, the 5-foot-9, 185-pounder faced the prospect of his football career ending before it even got started so many times that he eventually became immune to the notion. So where did it get him?

Well, in 2007, he established an NFL record for the most receptions by a player in his first year with a new team. His 112 catches with New England that season set a Patriots record and tied him for the league lead with T.J. Houshmandzadeh of the Cincinnati Bengals.

A year later, Welker caught 111 passes to rank No. 2 in the NFL behind the 115 passes hauled in by Andre Johnson of the Houston Texans.

Welker and the Patriots are a perfect fit. He proved with quarterbacks Tom Brady in 2007 and Matt Cassel in 2008 that regardless of who's pitching, Welker will find the open spot and make the catch. Move him inside or outside on offense, keep him back for punt returns or even kick returns and Welker will get the job done.

IN THE HUDDLE
Welker's 112 catches in 2007 set an NFL record for the most receptions by a player in his first season with a new team.

The Patriots haven't achieved their status of league superpower without knowing a thing or two about their opponents. So it was in Week 5 of 2004 that Welker, then a recent arrival with the Miami Dolphins, tweaked the interest of coach Bill Belichick and the Patriots when he took over the Dolphins' kicking duties from kicker Olindo Mare who sustained an injury in warmup.

Although New England won that game at Foxboro 24–10, Welker was named AFC special teams player of the week by becoming the first player in NFL history to a have a kickoff return, punt return, field goal (1-for-1 from 29 yards), successful point-after attempt and kickoff in the same game.

Then in Week 15 of 2004, Welker provided a 71-yard punt return during Miami's 29–28 upset

of the Patriots. Two years later, during a 20–10 Dolphin loss at New England, Welker set what was then a personal high with nine receptions.

The all-hustle, multi-talented Welker made such an impact on New England that on March 5, 2007 the Pats acquired him from the Dolphins for second round and seventh round selections in that year's draft.

Welker set career highs in 2007 with 1,175 receiving yards and eight touchdowns. At Super Bowl XLII, he tied the championship game's record with 11 receptions (for 103 yards) in the nail-biting loss to the New York Giants.

His 1,165 receiving yards in 2008 not only made Welker a first-time Pro Bowler, but also proved his previous campaign was no one-hit wonder. When he caught nine passes against the Buffalo Bills in Week 10 of 2008, Welker set an NFL record with six-or-more

receptions in his first nine games of the season. He extended his record to 11 games before a four-catch performance in Week 13.

Given all he's achieved, it's amazing he was overlooked by so many. Welker starred at Heritage High School in Oklahoma City and felt his development in football was assisted by his participation in soccer. Yet not one college recruited him, even after he and his family sent out more than 100 faxes in an attempt to get an opportunity.

He got to Texas Tech only because another player backed out of his commitment. But once there, he was nicknamed "The Natural" and emerged as one of that school's finest products. Still, he went undrafted in 2004, but did sign as a free agent with the San Diego Chargers.

Welker got through training camp only to be cut after playing one game with the Chargers. Along came Miami, where he fared well

CAREER HIGHLIGHTS

• Set a Patriots single-season reception record with 112 receptions in 2007.

• Second in receptions in 2008 with 111.

• Tied a Super Bowl record with 11 receptions in Super Bowl XLII.

• Named to the Pro Bowl in 2008.

over three seasons. Fortunately, the Patriots took notice and when he arrived Brady referred to Welker — respectfully — as a Labrador retriever for the way he'd fetch the ball, come back to the huddle panting and sweating and be ready to head out and catch again.

Coincidentally, Welker has a Lab named Nash, after star NBA guard Steve Nash. Like Nash the basketball player, the diminutive Welker has become a big man in his league.

RODDY WHITE

The 2008 NFL season offered a great leap for the Atlanta Falcons. Coming off a 4–12 year in 2007 in a season tainted by the off-field legal distractions of quarterback Michael Vick, the Falcons soared to a record of 11–5 in 2008 before falling to the Cinderella Arizona Cardinals in the post-season.

In addition to quarterback Matt Ryan arriving via the draft and running back Michael Turner landing through free agency, the Falcons also got a huge kickstart in

the right direction by the continued escalation of wide receiver Roddy White.

Sharod Lamor White was born in James Island, South Carolina, on November 2, 1981. Football, wrestling and baseball were his sporting pursuits at James Island High School, with the gridiron and wrestling mat providing state recognition for him. At the University of Alabama-Birmingham, White thrived even more, leading the collegiate ranks as a senior with 1,452 receiving yards. In 45 career games with the Blazers he recorded 3,112 receiving yards.

White was a backup in the first seven games of his NFL career. His first NFL start in Week 9 of 2005 produced three catches for 50 yards in a win at Miami. He scored his first TD the following week in a loss at Green Bay on a 19-yard toss from Vick.

Over his first two NFL seasons, White developed a case of the "dropsies" and was plagued by inconsistency that prompted some to suggest the Falcons fouled up in using a first round draft pick to corral him in 2005.

But after the final regular season game of 2008, where White made three catches for 48 yards and one touchdown, he basked in the glow of setting the Falcons record for receiving yards in a season with

1,382. He beat the previous record set by Alfred Jenkins in 1981 by 24 yards, and his 2008 total was fourth-best in the league. Most importantly, White noted back-to-back 1,000-plus yard seasons and his first Pro Bowl selection in 2008 erased for good all that initial talk about him being a bust.

IN THE HUDDLE
White's 1,202 yards receiving in 2007 made him the first Falcons receiver to compile a 1,000-yard season since Terance Mathis did it in 1999.

Moving forward, the onus should be on how high he takes his game and, in the process, just how good the Falcons can become. Aside from living with his on-field troubles at the outset, White did take some heat and absorbed a fine of $10,000 when he unveiled a T-shirt stating "Free Mike Vick" following one of his touchdowns in 2007. White felt it was important that Vick, his first pro QB, knew his friends hadn't abandoned him.

When 2007 came to a close, White became the first Falcon since 1999 to reach 1,000 receiving yards in a season, and 2008 made him the first Falcon with back-to-back 1,000 receiving-yard seasons since 1998–99 and the first Falcon to hurdle over 1,200 yards in successive seasons.

CAREER HIGHLIGHTS

- Pro Bowl selection in 2008.
- Ranked fourth in the NFL in receiving yards in 2008 with 1,382 yards.
- Drafted 27th overall from the University of Alabama-Birmingham by the Atlanta Falcons in 2005.
- Second all-time in UAB history with 163 receptions for 3,112 yards and 26 touchdowns.

All this was quite staggering, considering that over his first two NFL campaigns, he'd caught only 59 passes for 952 yards and three touchdowns. By 2007 he had 83 receptions for 1,202 yards and six touchdowns, and in 2008 his output totaled 88 receptions for 1,382 yards and seven touchdowns.

A determined competitor, White believes his career bottomed out before it went on a steady incline. He's developing into a wide receiver peers and fans really respect. What's more, the better the Falcons become, the more recognition he'll receive, especially with more games like the 30–24 playoff loss at Arizona where White caught a post-season franchise record 11 passes for 84 yards and one touchdown. Not bad for his first trip to the second season.

The 6-foot, 208-pound White has evolved over the years from starting eight games as rookie and five as a sophomore to starting 15 games in each of 2007 and 2008. His 100-plus yard receiving games have also risen, from one in each of his first two seasons to five in 2007 and seven in 2008.

White is a big-time pass-catching playmaker and one of the big reasons the Falcons are back in flight.

DALLAS COWBOYS
★ ★ ★

TIGHT END

82

JASON WITTEN

Jason Witten is not just a great tight end, he is also one of the toughest players in the entire NFL. Take for example a couple of moments during the Dallas Cowboys' 2008 season. During a Monday night contest against the Philadelphia Eagles, Witten separated his shoulder in the first half. But he was right back out after taking a pain-killing shot and finished the contest with seven receptions for a total of 110 yards. His biggest catch of the night came late in the fourth quarter when he nabbed a 32-yard pass and made it to the Eagles five-yard line, which set up a Marion Barber touchdown to give Dallas a 41–37 victory. Later in the 2008 campaign, Witten suffered a broken rib, but it only really affected him for one contest — he did not record a catch during a game against the New York Giants. Just three weeks later, Witten caught a season-high nine passes for 115 yards and one touchdown in a 34–9 win over the Seattle Seahawks. Even as a rookie Witten had showed a tougher mettle than most when he broke his jaw — requiring extensive repairs with three plates put in his face — and only missed one game in the 2003 season.

While teammates marvel at Witten's toughness and determination to play, he does not see it as big deal. He just says, "Make the repairs and send me back out there because the team needs me." The 6-foot-5, 265-pounder was one of the first players drafted by the organization when Bill Parcells was running the Cowboys. A native of Elizabethon, Tennessee, Witten attended the University of Tennessee and was recruited there as a defensive end. He switched to the tight end position soon afterward and he decided to leave the university after his junior year. He had compiled a record of 68 catches for 797 yards and that caught the eye of the Cowboys, who selected him 69th overall in 2003. He caught 35 passes as an NFL rookie, but then put up pass reception totals of 87, 66

CAREER HIGHLIGHTS

• Five-time Pro Bowl selection (2004–2008)

• In 2007 he became the first Cowboys tight end to have over 1,000 yards receiving.

• Caught 15 passes in a single game in 2007 for a Cowboys record.

• Became the only Cowboys tight end in history to have 60 receptions in four consecutive seasons.

and 64 over the next three years. His best season came in 2007 when he caught 96 passes, good for 1,145 yards and seven TDs. By the end of the 2008 season, Witten was a Pro Bowler for the fifth straight time — he was named to the starting roster for the 2009 contest — and is one the most reliable receivers on the Cowboys offense. His 81 receptions in 2008 were more than high-profile teammate Terrell Owens' total of 69. It was the second year in a row Witten had hauled in more catches than the always-loud Owens.

IN THE HUDDLE

Witten established a Cowboys record for tight ends with 96 catches in 2007.

Dallas quarterback Tony Romo says Witten does it all for the Cowboys — run, catch and block. The durable Witten (he has missed only one game since joining the Cowboys) is just entering his prime years since he is only 26 years old. Early in the 2009 season he will pass the 5,000-yard mark for receptions and he has only played 95 career games. Witten is so good at his position because he can run excellent routes and has very soft hands. Once he gets his mitts on the ball he is very difficult to bring down because he is as big as a linebacker and can easily take on the toughest of defensive backs. Witten's presence in the Dallas attack allows the other talented players to do their work because he often draws double coverage. But when it's all on the line, you can bet Romo feels most comfortable going to his big tight end for the important passing plays. Witten is also like a sixth offensive lineman when he lines up to block and that helps Dallas run the ball along the ground.

An injury to Romo put a heavy dent in the Cowboys' plans to make the playoffs in 2008. Dallas got off to a great start, winning four of their first five contests, but was only able to finish with a 7–9 record in a very tough NFC East Division. If the Cowboys are to get back in the post-season, Romo must stay healthy and have Witten play to his usual high standard. Witten may get some help at his position if the 6-foot-6, 253-pound Martellus Bennett continues to develop as a tight end (he caught 23 passes in 2008). Any assistance for the sure-handed Witten is bound to keep him fresher and ready to make the tough plays needed to win a football game.

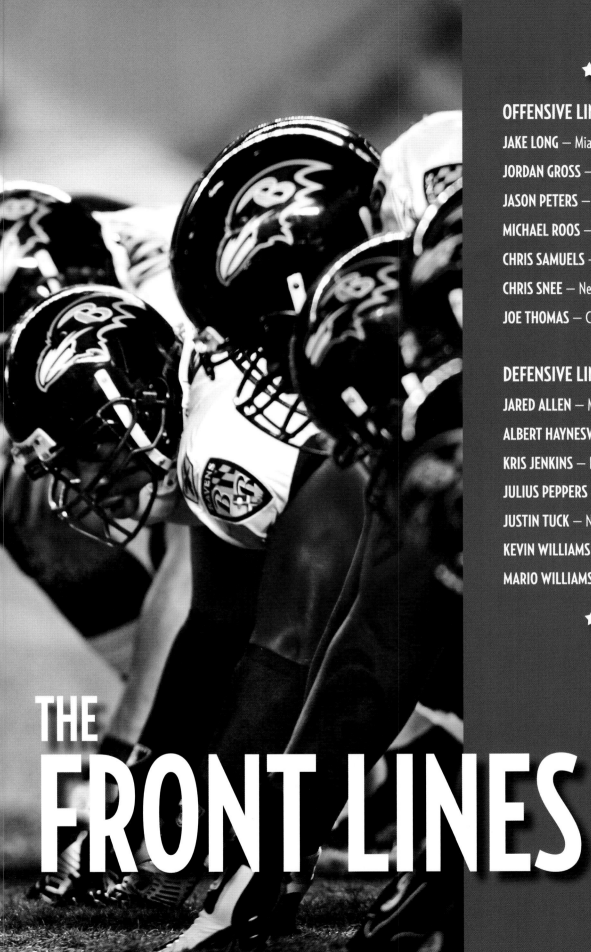

OFFENSIVE LINEMEN:

JAKE LONG — Miami Dolphins

JORDAN GROSS — Carolina Panthers

JASON PETERS — Philadelphia Eagles

MICHAEL ROOS — Tennessee Titans

CHRIS SAMUELS — Washington Redskins

CHRIS SNEE — New York Giants

JOE THOMAS — Cleveland Browns

DEFENSIVE LINEMEN:

JARED ALLEN — Minnesota Vikings

ALBERT HAYNESWORTH — Washington Redskins

KRIS JENKINS — New York Jets

JULIUS PEPPERS — Carolina Panthers

JUSTIN TUCK — New York Giants

KEVIN WILLIAMS — Minnesota Vikings

MARIO WILLIAMS — Houston Texans

THE
FRONT LINES

JAKE LONG

A funny thing happened to Jake Long as he was developing to become the first overall selection of the 2008 NFL draft — he nearly died.

Early in the summer of 2004, Long was awakened sometime between 3 and 4 a.m. to the reality that the house he was sharing with 10 other Michigan Wolverine players was burning to the ground. The 6-foot-7, 315-pound offensive lineman tried to get out the door of his room, but quickly realized the fire was raging just outside it. Given no other option, he leapt through the window of his second story room and landed on top of a 1980 Ford Bronco that had a high roof.

Long did not have far to fall, but he was still very lucky not to break any bones. Despite the fact he was coughing and throwing up due to smoke inhalation, Long insisted to authorities that he was fine. They eventually convinced him to go to a hospital, where he was quickly put on a respirator and was at one point fighting for his life. However, his big, strong body allowed him to overcome the problems and within three weeks, he was back to getting ready for football. Long was determined not to let the harrowing incident slow him down and he developed an appreciation for how life can change so quickly.

By the time the 2008 draft rolled around, Long was rated one of the best prospects available. He could have left school after his junior year at Michigan, but was only projected as a possible third-rounder at that point. He felt an obligation to finish out his college career and the Wolverines were certainly happy to keep their star lineman, although a shot at a national title was ruined with a couple of unexpected losses.

IN THE HUDDLE

During Long's three years as a starter at Lapeer East High School he allowed zero sacks and became the first player in school history to earn first-team all-state honors.

By virtue of their inept 1–15 record in 2007, the Miami Dolphins were slated to draft first overall in 2008. They looked at trading their pick in exchange for a slew of lower selections, but when the Dolphins realized they were not going to get what they wanted in any swap, negotiations with Long's agent began. Miami's new GM Jeff Ireland insisted Long was always on top of their list and the newly appointed head coach Tony Sparano thought Long had all the necessary skills to be a top NFL lineman. Bill Parcells, who hired both Ireland and Sparano after taking over as executive vice-president of football operations for the Dolphins, is well known for liking big men along the line. He also wants players who allow his teams to build from the ground up and there was little doubt Long could be a long-term building

block. Ensuring there would be no holdout, the Dolphins signed Long to a five-year contract worth a total of $57.75 million with $30 million guaranteed.

Long played in all 16 games for the surprising Dolphins, who won their division in 2008 with an 11–5 record. Even though Miami lost its only playoff game, it was still a remarkable turnaround for the franchise. There were some difficult moments for the rookie, who had a rough game against the New York Jets in the season opener and then rolled his ankle later in the season. Still, he did not miss a game.

It was much easier for Long to dominate in college, where he could bull-rush an opposing defensive lineman with little trouble. However, in the NFL he had to face a quality player every game. He was able to hold his own in most contests, including with St. Louis defensive end Chris Long, the No. 2 pick in the 2008 draft.

Long dedicated himself to getting better at all aspects of his game, especially his pass-blocking techniques. The Dolphins line allowed just 25 sacks in 2008, but was not as good running the ball as it would have liked.

Dave DeGuglielmo, formerly of the New York Giants, has been hired as offensive line coach for the 2009 campaign and he comes with a reputation for building a solid running game. Long will be vital in getting the Dolphins offense to produce more in the future and being named to the Pro Bowl as a rookie should give him all the confidence he needs to become a more dominating player.

CAREER HIGHLIGHTS

- Two-time consensus All-American (2006, 2007) at Michigan University.
- Only one of 11 players in school history to be elected captain at least twice during their careers at Michigan.
- Named to the 2009 Pro Bowl; Long is the first No.1 pick to be named to the Pro Bowl in his rookie season since George Rogers of the New Orleans Saints did it in 1981.

JORDAN GROSS

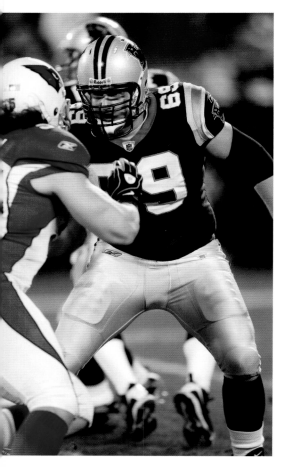

Offensive linemen, once the forgotten group in NFL circles, are garnering more attention in this day and age. Their salaries reflect their rise in importance and an example of that occurred in 2008 when the Carolina Panthers designated offensive tackle Jordan Gross their franchise player and signed him to a one-year contract for $7.45 million.

As if on cue, Gross responded with another strong, progressive campaign that culminated with his selection to the Pro Bowl and gaining the most votes (34) in the All-Pro tabulation among offensive tackles (Tennessee's Michael Roos was next with 32).

True, running back DeAngelo Williams established a Titans record by galloping to 1,515 yards on the ground. But as a team, the Panthers in 2008 established a club high for rushing yards in a season with 2,437 — which ranked third-best in the league — tied for second in the league in rushing yardage per carry (4.8) and bettered the club record for rushing TDs in a season from 17 to 30. The Panthers were seventh in the NFL with an average of 25.9 points per game in 2008, in large part by playing the run first and the pass second.

Carolina's O-line gained much credit for the results, and that is a testament to the entire unit, given that not one of the starters played in all 16 games. The club's final regular season game of 2008 saw 28-year-old Gross at left tackle, 22-year-old Jeff Otah at right tackle, 23-year-old Ryan Kalil at center, 30-year-old Keydrick Vincent at right guard and 27-year-old Travelle Wharton at left guard. The unit, it's fair to say, is hardly over the hill.

Given Gross' sure-fire development, he fully justified the Panthers' decision to select him third overall in 2003. He left Utah as a consensus all-American, finalist for the Outland Trophy — given annually to the best interior lineman in the NCAA — and without surrendering a sack in his final two seasons.

Aside from his prowess in football, Gross obtained his black belt in tae-kwon-do while attending Fruitland High School in his home state of Idaho. Given the fierce battles that occur along football lines, such training can only help Gross in his attempts to ward off or create holes against hulking defensive lineman and charging linebackers.

At 12–4 in 2008, Carolina equaled the New York Giants on record, but had to settle for the No. 2 seed in the NFC. The Panthers then defied logic and bombed out on a mistake-prone day against the surprising Arizona Cardinals in the post-season. It was a bitter way to end a sweet season. For Gross, there was one more game. He'd made his first trip to Hawaii as a 20-year-old on his honeymoon. In February 2009 he was back — as a Pro Bowler.

CAREER HIGHLIGHTS

- Selected to Pro Bowl in 2008.
- Drafted 8th overall from the University of Utah by the Carolina Panthers in 2003.
- Only rookie starter on offensive line that established a Panthers team record by yielding only 27 sacks in 2003.
- Has started every game he has played in the NFL (95 games).

JASON PETERS

Jason Peters felt he deserved a new deal from the Buffalo Bills before the start of the 2008 season. After all, he had given the team a Pro Bowl performance in 2007 and worked very hard to make himself one of the best left tackles in football. Peters also knew the Bills were going into the season uncertain as to how quarterback Trent Edwards was going to fare in his second full year at the helm. They were counting on a strong line that had allowed only 26 sacks in 2007 to protect him.

The Bills would not move off their position that Peters had a signed contract (with a base salary of $3.25 million) and wouldn't even discuss the possibility of a new deal unless he reported to the team. He finally caved in early September and although Peters was unhappy about playing under his old contract, his presence instantly made the Bills a better team.

Living up to the reputation of being a Pro Bowl player can be difficult, but the task becomes even more daunting when an entire training camp is missed. The Bills were also implementing a new offense complete with different terminology and the team was concerned Peters might not be ready for the long season. However, he was able to shake off the rust pretty quickly. Peters is a strong believer in the running game and he soon had the faith of Bills offensive coordinator Turk Schonert. Not long into the season, the Bills could honestly say Peters had reached the level of consistency he had shown a year ago.

It was never easy, however, as the Bills had an up-and-down campaign that saw them finish 7–9 in 2008. At one point they looked like a sure playoff team, but faded in the second half to miss the postseason once again. The best part of Buffalo's attack over the entire season was the running game. Peters and his mates along the line opened holes for Marshawn Lynch (who rushed for 1,036 yards) and Fred Jackson (who gained 571 yards). There were some early criticisms of Peters, but by the end of 2008 he was a Pro Bowl selection — even after missing three games. Despite the about-face of Peters' dedication to the Buffalo's offensive system, the Bills decided it was time to part ways with the tackle, after the two sides could not reach an agreement on a new contract. Peters was sent to the Philadelphia Eagles in exchange for a 2009 first round draft pick, and was given all the financial security he needed with a six-year $60-million pact.

CAREER HIGHLIGHTS

- Pro Bowl selection in 2007 and 2008.
- Has scored two NFL touchdowns: a pass from J.P. Losman in 2005 and a blocked punt in 2004.
- Signed by the Bills as an undrafted free agent in 2004; was released in August 2004 but then re-signed to the practice squad before being signed to the active roster in November 2004.

MICHAEL ROOS

Mihkel Roos is now living in what once seemed a fairytale when he lived in poverty over the first 10 years of his life in Tallinn, Estonia. His mother worked two jobs attempting to make ends meet. Then a year after the demise of the Soviet Union, she picked up her three children and moved to Vancouver, Washington.

CAREER HIGHLIGHTS

- Pro Bowl selection in 2008.
- Has started every game in his five-year career since being drafted in 2005.
- Signed a six-year, $43-million contract extension with the Titans in April 2008.

Living in his aunt's home, in a new country with a new opportunity, Mihkel became known as Michael. He showed multi-sport talent in football, basketball and track and field (javelin). One season of playing tight end and on the defensive line in high school produced a scholarship to Eastern Washington University. He redshirted for a year in football and basketball before electing to pursue life on the football field.

A year on the defensive line was followed by a switch to the offensive line. His performance in the Senior Bowl in 2005 attracted much attention. When the Tennessee Titans selected him 41st overall in the second round of that year's draft he scored an NFL-best for his alma mater.

As he entered his fourth NFL season, Roos signed a six-year contract extension with the Titans. He's maintained his hometown connection with Vancouver and in the process he's also become a pillar for Tennessee's splendid offensive line. Believed to be the first NFL player from Estonia, Roos was voted All-Pro and a Pro Bowler in 2008, when the Titans posted the NFL's finest record at 13–3.

The O-line played a huge part in that success, recovering after the loss of guards Benji Olson, who retired, and Jacobi Bell, who left via free agency. With Roos at left tackle, the ever-rambunctious David Stewart at right tackle and three-time All-Pro Kevin Mawae at center, the unit didn't skip a beat with new guards Jake Scott and Eugene Amano.

Tennessee's 12 sacks allowed matched Denver for the fewest in the NFL in 2008 and improved from a total of 30 sacks allowed the previous season. In the process, rookie running back Chris Johnson rushed for 1,228 yards and the club ranked seventh in rushing overall. Meanwhile, drop-back passer Kerry Collins was allowed to thrive in the pocket, thanks to the excellent pass protection.

Roos is invaluable to the mix considering his blocking handles the blindside for Collins. At 6-foot-7 and 315 pounds, Roos is an imposing figure showing signs of excellence like another franchise great, Hall of Famer Bruce Matthews.

CHRIS SAMUELS

WASHINGTON REDSKINS

★ ★ ★

OFFENSIVE TACKLE

60

It speaks to how respected a player is when, even in a season when he's hampered by injuries and his club misses the playoffs, he still gains recognition. Such was the case for Washington Redskins left offensive tackle Chris Samuels in 2008.

Hobbled by a bum knee that eventually caused him to miss one game, then missing the final three games because of a torn right triceps, Samuels still earned his sixth Pro Bowl selection. That allowed him to equal center Len Hauss, who'd set the franchise record for Pro Bowl selections by a Redskins offensive lineman.

Unfortunately, the triceps injury prevented Samuels from playing in Honolulu, his withdrawal paving the way for the addition of New Orleans tackle Jammal Brown. But at age 31, the 6-foot-5, 317-pound Samuels remained a key component of the Redskins.

Born in Mobile, Alabama, and a product of the Alabama Crimson Tide, Samuels was one of two picks the Redskins had among the top three in the 2000 NFL draft. The Penn State duo of defensive end Courtney Brown (to Cleveland) and linebacker LaVar Arrington (to Washington via New Orleans) went one-two. Samuels went No. 3 in a pick the Redskins obtained from San Francisco.

Samuels captured the Outland Trophy in 1999 as the outstanding college interior lineman. It was a season where his blocking helped Shaun Alexander gain 1,383 yards for Bama and it brought a remarkable end to his college career with a streak of 42 games without allowing a sack.

A skilled pass protector and steady run blocker, Samuels plays with an edge that has seen rivals accuse him of dirty tactics. He was fined for delivering an illegal chop block during a game against the Bears in 2007 and later apologized. He also fended off a claim of intent to injure by the Giants' Mathias Kiwanuka in 2008.

While rivals feel his intensity, his teammates admire him. On his 31st birthday, a video of a prank his teammates staged made it to the Internet. To the delight of many, Samuels took the large birthday cake prepared for the occasion right in the face.

The Redskins have been more than delighted with their offensive tackles for the past decade in Samuels and Jon Jansen. There are concerns Jansen, 32, and Samuels, 31, are succumbing to the rigors of their trade with age. The Pro Bowl status maintained by Samuels in 2008 defied such speculation, with the Redskins expecting more in the years ahead.

CAREER HIGHLIGHTS

- Six-time Pro Bowl selection (2001, 2002, 2005–2008).
- His four consecutive Pro Bowl appearances are the most by a Redskin offensive lineman since Joe Jacoby and Russ Grimm accomplished the feat between 1983–86.
- Has started in 136 regular season games with the Washington Redskins.

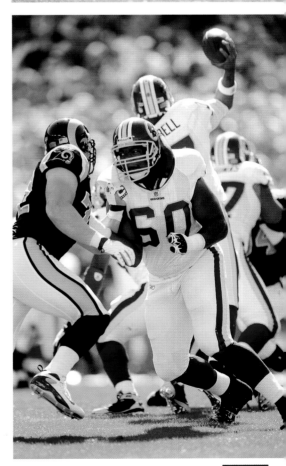

NEW YORK GIANTS
★ ★ ★
OFFENSIVE GUARD
76

CHRIS SNEE

When the New York Giants signed right guard Chris Snee to a new six-year contract worth $43.5 million, they made sure the offensive line that helped win Super Bowl XLII would remain in tact at least until 2012. Left tackle David Diehl is locked up until 2013, as is left guard Rich Seubert, while right tackle Kareem McKenzie and center Shaun O'Hara have deals that cover them until 2012.

Snee's new pact will take him to 2014. The Giants have built their offense around this gifted group of linemen who genuinely like each other and enjoy preparing for games as a unit. Their ability to work together and get along virtually assures they will be a cohesive unit for the foreseeable future and gives New York a chance to contend year in and year out.

Considering Snee was a second round pick out of Boston College in 2004, he has likely surpassed all expectations. He started 11 games in 2004 before an injury prematurely ended his year. Since then, he has started 64 consecutive games. Snee not only plays well, he gets the job done without taking many penalties; he was called for only three holding calls during the entire 2008 season. The Giants have one the best running games in the NFL and a marquee quarterback in Eli Manning to go along with their highly efficient offensive line, anchored by Snee. League-wide recognition has been elusive for New York's O-line, but that finally changed when Snee was voted to the Pro Bowl as a starter for his performance in 2008, while O'Hara was named as a reserve.

Giants head coach Tom Coughlin was happy to see Snee get the money and Pro Bowl nomination since the 6-foot-3, 317-pound guard is not only a valuable part of his team, but also his son-in-law. Snee married Coughlin's daughter, Katie, and that marriage has produced two grandchildren for the Giants mentor. The player certainly gets needled by his teammates for his closeness to the coach, but Snee takes it all in stride. He refers to his father-in-law as "coach" and gets to see a side of Coughlin few have a chance to observe. Both are able to keep the personal and professional relationships separate and the coach emphasizes Snee is on the team because he is a tough, physical competitor who takes a lunch-bucket approach to his job. Anyone who watches Snee perform on a week-to-week basis would arrive at the same conclusion.

CAREER HIGHLIGHTS

- 2008 Pro Bowl Selection.
- His 64-game playing streak is the third among active Giant players behind Eli Manning (71) and David Diehl (96).
- Integral part of an offense that helped the Giants score 373 points in 2007, the fifth highest in franchise history.
- Signed a six-year, $41.25-million contract extension in June 2008.

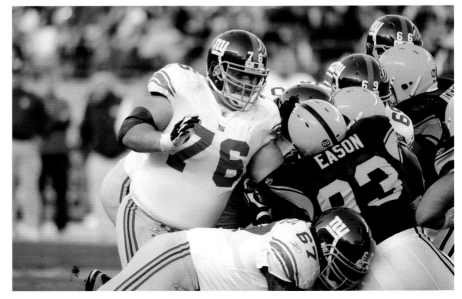

JOE THOMAS

It is one of the most unglamorous positions in all of football, yet one of the most important. No team can win without a top offensive tackle who can protect the blind side of the quarterback. When the Cleveland Browns had a chance to select a potential all-star at this crucial position, they did not hesitate to take 6-foot-6, 305-pound Joe Thomas third overall in the 2007 NFL draft.

With his Pro Bowl selection in 2008, Thomas appears ready for stardom and at the age of 23 will likely be the best player at his position for years to come. The Browns finally have a cornerstone to build their offense around.

Cleveland hasn't always fared so well with high picks in the draft. Quarterback Tim Couch, defensive end Courtney Brown and defensive tackle Gerard Brown are good examples of how poorly the organization drafted between 1999 and 2001. The selection of Thomas gave the Browns a solid anchor for their offensive line and he believes he can lead one of the best lines in the NFL. It certainly worked out well in 2007 when the Browns went 10–6 in his rookie year, but not so well in 2008 when Cleveland was a huge disappointment at 4–12. However, there is no way the poor record could be pinned on the performance of players like Thomas, who was stellar in a bad year for the team.

Thomas is very quick for a big man and that helps him deal with speedy pass rushers. He also can play a straight-ahead game that allows him to manage those who use shear force to overwhelm an offensive lineman. Thomas has shown himself to be mature and able to deal with the ups and downs of playing such an important position. His easygoing demeanor appeals to his teammates and he certainly does not take himself too seriously. For instance, he went fishing with his dad the day of the NFL draft. He does thrive on the challenge of playing an important role on his team.

Other teams are so envious of what Thomas has accomplished in such as short time that eight clubs took offensive tackles with first round draft choices in 2008. Time will tell if they are successful with their selections, but there is no doubt new Browns coach Eric Mangini will be counting on the all-star tackle to lead his offense back to respectability.

CAREER HIGHLIGHTS

- Two-time Pro Bowl selection (2007, 2008).
- Has started every game for the Browns since being drafted third overall from the University of Wisconsin in 2007.
- Was runner up to Adrian Peterson as 2007 offensive rookie of the year.
- Helped anchor a line which only allowed 24 sacks in 2008, ranking the Browns eighth in the NFL.

JARED ALLEN

The Minnesota Vikings knew they were getting one of the best defensive ends in the NFL when they made a deal with the Kansas City Chiefs to acquire 6-foot-6, 270-pound Jared Allen. Coming off a season that saw Allen record a league-high 15.5 quarterback sacks in 2007, the Vikings gave their prized acquisition a whopping six-year deal worth a total of $73.3 million dollars. Minnesota's management was very thorough in researching Allen's background and came away convinced they were making the right move by trading the 17th overall pick in the 2008 NFL draft to the Chiefs, along with a pair of third round choices. By the end of the 2008 campaign, the Vikings were very happy with their decision.

It is only natural observers would ask why the Chiefs decided to divest themselves of such a good player. It is something of an understatement to say Kansas City management was less than thrilled with Allen's off-field comportment.

His mixing of drinking and driving led the Chiefs to believe he would always be too wild for their liking. However, Allen himself came to the conclusion he need to reform his ways, which meant he abstained from drinking alcohol and stayed firm to a commitment about staying out of places that had landed him in trouble previously. Allen changed his attitude and diet to reflect his new approach after realizing his dream of playing in the NFL — something he first thought about as an eight-year-old — was seriously at risk.

Allen quickly made the Vikings defensive line one the best in football. His presence made better players of defensive tackles Pat Williams and Kevin Williams, and he was a great leader for the Vikings in the locker room, despite not being able to limit his on-field indiscretions, which cost him about $90,000 in fines, mostly for late hits. Vikings head coach Brad Childress thinks Allen plays the run and pass with equal effectiveness and the rugged defender has a never-say-die attitude. He recorded 14.5 quarterback sacks in 2008, the fifth-highest total in the league, while playing in all 16 games. His performance earned him a spot on the Pro Bowl team, a fitting reward for the reformed star. Allen's level of play was even more remarkable considering he had to play with a bad shoulder for most the year and a knee injury late in the season.

CAREER HIGHLIGHTS

- Recorded two safeties in 2008 to lead the NFL.
- In 2006 led the NFL in fumbles recovered with six.
- Two-time Pro Bowl selection (2007, 2008).
- Drafted 126th overall from Idaho State by the Kansas City Chiefs in 2004.

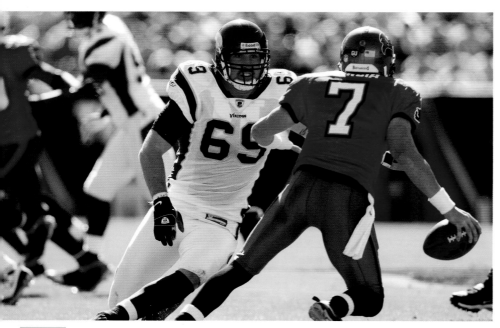

ALBERT HAYNESWORTH

WASHINGTON REDSKINS
★ ★ ★
DEFENSIVE TACKLE
92

It was one of the ugliest incidents in NFL history and it got Washington Redskins defensive tackle Albert Haynesworth an unprecedented five-game suspension. During a 2006 contest against Dallas, Haynesworth, a member of the Tennessee Titans at the time, stepped on the face of Cowboy Andre Gourde after the latter's helmet had come off his head. It caused a gash that took 30 stitches to close and gave Haynesworth notoriety he could have lived without.

The 6-foot-6, 320-pound lineman knew he had done something terrible and called Gourde to apologize. The question then became could Haynesworth, a first round draft choice of the Titans in 2002, learn to control his rage on the field and make himself an effective player? If the last two seasons are any indication, Haynesworth has indeed reformed himself into a top-notch defender. The Washington Redskins are certainly believers; why else would they have handed him a seven-year, $100-million contract ($41 million guaranteed) in February of 2009?

One of the best things that happened to Haynesworth was the interest taken in him by former NFL player Chuck Smith. A defensive lineman for the Atlanta Falcons, Smith was also a Tennessee Volunteer in his college

days, just like Haynesworth. Smith took a shine to the troubled Titan and spent time coaching him on techniques he could use to rush the quarterback and offered a good dose of advice on how to conduct himself. He was also able to work on his conditioning and Haynesworth got the message that he had to re-invent himself.

Haynesworth's game is built around his strength, immense size and an ability to wreak havoc against any offense. He is very athletic for a man of his stature and can take on double teams and still come out on top. Haynesworth can clog the middle of the line with great effectiveness and is fast enough to play like a defensive end. He could hardly last an entire game when he first started with the Titans, but he is now a much more dedicated player. He was the most important member of the Titans defense and the strategy of moving him around, along the line, only served to make the opposition worry more about the All-Pro defender.

Through counseling, Haynesworth has been able to control his emotions on the field. However, the intensity is still there and that led to a great year in 2008, which saw him record a career-high 8.5 quarterback sacks. In addition, he had 22 quarterback pressures and his tremendous play helped Tennessee win 13 games in 2008, equaling a club record.

CAREER HIGHLIGHTS

- Selected to the Pro Bowl twice (2007, 2008).
- In 2007 led all AFC defensive tackles with six sacks; was tied for fifth in the NFL among defensive tackles.
- Forced a career-high three fumbles in 2008.
- Drafted 15th overall from the University of Tennessee by the Tennessee Titans in 2002.

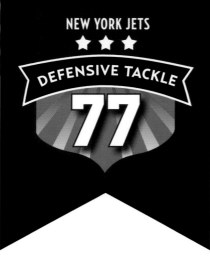

DEFENSIVE TACKLE
77

KRIS JENKINS

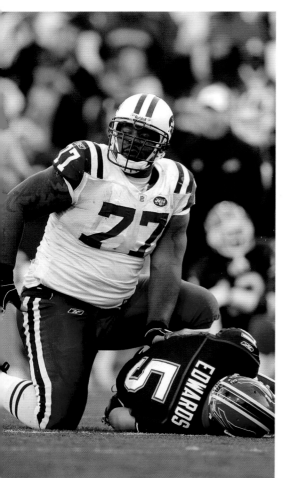

CAREER HIGHLIGHTS

• Four-time Pro Bowl selection (2002, 2003, 2006, 2008).

• The first defensive lineman in Panthers history to appear in the Pro Bowl.

• His three blocked kicks tie him with Michael Bates for most in Carolina history.

At one time, defensive tackle Kris Jenkins feared his life was in peril from being too heavy. Injuries to his shoulder and knee ligaments limited the second round draft choice — taken 44th overall in 2001— of the Carolina Panthers to just five games between 2004 and 2005. His weight ballooned to well over 400 pounds and even though he returned to play 16 games in 2006, the Panthers viewed their nose tackle as expendable. He was ear marked for a trade despite the fact he had started 11 games as a rookie and recorded seven quarterback sacks in just his second year with Carolina.

Luckily for Jenkins, the New York Jets were willing to spend second and fifth round draft choices to acquire him after the 2007 campaign. The Jets knew Jenkins was not in the best of shape and the status of his knee was questionable. They gambled he would find his game in their 3–4 alignment, even though Jenkins was already struggling in a 3–4 and had the likes of Julius Peppers beside him in Carolina. As the season wore on it was clear the Jets made the right call. Jenkins showed his size and athletic prowess were still valuable weapons. He recorded 3.5 sacks during the 2008 season and earned a third career nomination to the Pro Bowl.

Jenkins proved to be a positive influence on his new teammates and was very willing to make others look good, not caring about personal statistics. He was up to the challenge of a new role in a 3–4, which meant he was often double-teamed. Jenkins knows the position of nose tackle is not very glamorous, but realizes size — he's now down to a more manageable 350 pounds over his 6-foot-4 frame — and intensity are required to do the job effectively.

Jenkins was able to play all 16 games for New York and was very grateful to the Jets for giving him a chance to redeem himself as an NFL star. He was very pleased to play for former Jets coach Eric Mangini, and realizes new bench boss Rex Ryan may make new demands. No doubt, he is now ready for any challenge put in this path.

The former Maryland player is used to dealing with tough realities since he grew up in a single-parent household with his father and brother Cullen. As a youngster he was put in charge of cooking and he quickly learned to fix a variety meals. It's no wonder then that Jenkins can adapt to any situation.

JULIUS PEPPERS

Julius Peppers' sack totals have been in double digits over most of his eight-year NFL career. But in 2007, the defensive end recorded a mere 2.5 sacks and the Carolina Panthers finished with a mediocre 7–9 record and out of the playoffs. Knowing he needed to rededicate himself, Peppers spent the off-season training at the Athletes' Performance Institute in Tempe, Arizona. Being away from the Panthers training facilities was also of benefit as Peppers was able to escape everything and just focus on preparing for the 2008 season. The change of scenery did a world of good for the 6-foot-6, 283-pounder, who worked on his speed and strength, hitting the weight room with enthusiasm. He came back refreshed and his teammates and the rest of the NFL took notice.

By the time the 2008 season was over, Peppers had recorded 14.5 sacks and was named as a starter to the Pro Bowl team, marking the fourth time in his career he was named to the squad. The Panthers were back in the playoffs with an NFC South Division-leading 12–4 record. The healthy and renewed Peppers was back to causing havoc on opposition offenses that had to face the defensive end they knew from years before.

At his best, Peppers is quick enough to disrupt plays before they even form in the backfield. He keeps the opposition guessing by lining up in different positions and when he is at the top of his pass-rushing game, he can take over a contest. He is often double- or triple-teamed, but understands his high level of play gets him that attention; he is very adept at shedding more than one attacker. Peppers was also more vocal than ever in 2008 — a change for the normally private player.

The second overall selection by the Panthers in 2002, Peppers has lived all of his life in North Carolina. He was raised in the small town of Bailey and then attended the University of North Carolina. Peppers left college after his junior year and recorded 12 sacks as a rookie in 2002. In 2004 he played in the Super Bowl when the Panthers were edged out by the New England Patriots. Peppers main goal is to win a Super Bowl, and by placing the franchise tag on the defensive end for 2009 season, the Panthers are hoping to get at least one more shot at going the distance with Peppers.

CAREER HIGHLIGHTS

- Ranks first in Panthers history with 70.5 sacks and 25 forced fumbles.
- 2002 NFL defensive rookie of the year.
- Four-time Pro Bowl selection (2004, 2005, 2006, 2008).
- One of three NFL players to record three sacks and one interception in the same game: Dallas, 2002.

NEW YORK GIANTS
★ ★ ★

DEFENSIVE END

91

JUSTIN TUCK

Winning programs tend to ride their veterans for as long as possible while wisely allowing younger understudies the opportunity to develop. Justin Tuck is a case in point. A third round draft pick of the New York Giants in 2005, the star defensive end with the Fighting Irish of Notre Dame started once in 14 games as a rookie, none in six games the following season

CAREER HIGHLIGHTS

- Recorded a career-high 12 sacks in 2008; good for seventh in the NFL.
- Selected to the 2008 Pro Bowl.
- In 2007, Tuck, Michael Strahan and Osi Umenyiora became the second trio in Giants history to record at least nine sacks each.

and twice over 16 games in 2007.

That was no slight on the swift, agile and remarkably strong 6-foot-5, 274-pounder from Kellyton in Coosa County, Alabama. He was merely paying his dues behind starters Michael Strahan and Osi Umenyiora, the former a marquee player, the latter a rising standout.

Yet Tuck saw increased game time in 2007, recording 10 sacks and 65 tackles. Those numbers clearly emphasized the Giants had their slot on the depth chart filled once Strahan retired after the triumph of Super Bowl XLII.

Some prognosticators wavered on the Giants at the beginning of 2008 because of Strahan's departure and the loss of Umenyiora for the entire season following knee surgery. But in what was the final

year of defensive coordinator Steve Spagnuolo's two seasons with the Giants, the club's defense actually moved up two spots from seventh in 2007 with 305 yards surrendered per game to fifth with 292 yards allowed per match.

Although their sacks total dropped from a league-leading 53 in 2007 to a sixth-best 42 in 2008, Tuck was tied for fourth among defensive lineman in sacks (12.0) and tackles (67). In Week 2 at St. Louis, Tuck's first NFL interception was memorable beyond his wildest dreams, as he showed uncanny speed to race 41 yards for a touchdown. He became a first-time All-Pro and Pro Bowler, doing his share in the Giants securing the NFC's No. 1 seed.

Tuck's championship ring matched his with his cousin Adalius Thomas, who celebrated an NFL title with the Baltimore Ravens in Super Bowl XXXV, coincidentally over the Giants.

Tuck, the second-youngest of seven children, excelled in football, basketball and baseball at Central County Coosa High School in Kellyton. The Tuck family presence is apparent among the 218 residents of Kellyton, a place Justin says has been referred to as "Tuckville." Tuck had 16 cousins in his high school graduating class and he made them proud when he left Kellyton for Notre Dame. Now that he is a Super Bowl champion, the town couldn't be happier — neither can the Giants.

KEVIN WILLIAMS

Kevin Williams and Pat Williams are no relation to each other, but they are quite the brotherhood when it comes to interior defensive linemen who bring an opponent's running game to a complete stop.

Nicknamed the "Williams Wall," this duo gave the Vikings the No. 1 defense against the run in 2006, 2007 and 2008, allowing a paltry average of 61.6, 74.1 and 76.9 yards per game over those seasons. At 6-foot-5 and 311 pounds, Kevin, No. 93, is the lighter of the two as Pat, No. 94, packs a reported 317 pounds on his 6-foot-3 frame.

Pat Williams was a free agent signing by the Vikings in 2005 and by that time Kevin had already endeared himself with Minnesota fans after two incredible seasons. Selected No. 9 overall out of Oklahoma State in 2003, Kevin Williams debuted at defensive end for the Vikings that year. The accomplishment made him only the third Vikings rookie defensive end to start the season opener.

After 12 games on the outside, Williams was moved inside as he put the finishing touches on a freshman campaign that produced a team-leading 10.5 sacks. His play attracted NFL all-rookie team recognition.

Williams' hometown is Fordyce, Arkansas, but he isn't the first from that city of just under 5,000 to acquire fame in football.

Paul "Bear" Bryant, the legendary coach at Alabama, also came out of Fordyce.

An outdoorsman who enjoys hunting and fishing, Williams was a two-way performer at Fordyce High, starring at tight end and on the line. His years at Oklahoma State resulted in improvement for the Cowboys. Their drive to the Houston Bowl in 2002 saw Williams selected the game's defensive MVP after his seven-tackle, three-sack performance against Southern Mississippi.

Over his first six NFL seasons, Williams played 94 of a possible 96 regular season games, missing two in 2005 with a knee injury. Given the double-teaming and pounding he endures in the trenches, Williams has shown remarkable durability.

Williams had a multi-interception season in 2007, returning both his picks for TDs, including one for 54 yards in the opening quarter of Week 1 against Atlanta. That was Minnesota's first major score of the season. However, the Williams Wall faced a stiff test

in December 2008 when Pat and Kevin were each handed four-game suspensions for violating the NFL's substance abuse policy. Claiming their innocence in using a diuretic, both linemen appealed and were able to play after receiving an injunction from a federal judge.

The Vikings signed Williams to a seven-year contract extension in 2006. It is Minnesota's hope that his 8.5 sacks in 2008 can be pushed back up toward his career-best 11.5, which he attained in 2004.

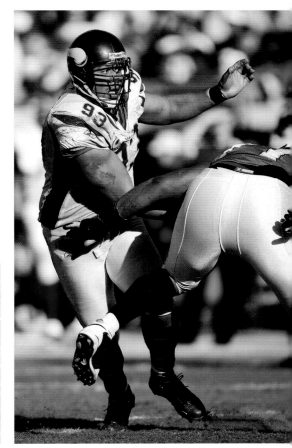

CAREER HIGHLIGHTS

- Four-time Pro Bowl selection (2004, 2006–2008).
- Led all defensive tackles in 2004 with 11.5 sacks.
- Only the second rookie in Vikings history to start every game.

HOUSTON TEXANS
★ ★ ★

DEFENSIVE END
90

MARIO WILLIAMS

CAREER HIGHLIGHTS

- Named the NFL player of the week in Week 1 in 2007.
- Named to his first Pro Bowl in 2008.
- Broke the record for career sacks at North Carolina State with 26.5 sacks.
- Named to Sports Illustrated's All-America Team in 2005.

The Houston Texans were a very bad football team during the 2005 NFL season, finishing the year with a terrible 2–14 record. The only good thing about their record was that it gave them the privilege of making the first selection in the 2006 draft. Most football experts thought the Texans would either take running back David Bush with their pick or a young quarterback like hometown boy Vince Young or Matt Leinhart. However, Houston management had other ideas and looked closely at who the main competition would be in their division. With quarterback Peyton Manning of the Indianapolis Colts — a team the Texans had never beaten in eight attempts — dominating the AFC South Division, the Texans determined they needed a defense that could stifle a high-powered offense. The Texans knew they badly needed a pass-rusher and made 6-foot-6, 283-pound defensive end Mario Williams the first pick in the draft. Williams was a somewhat unheralded performer coming off his junior year at North Carolina State and the Texans faced the heat of making a controversial first overall pick. But after three years of witnessing the big lineman grow and develop into a Pro Bowl starter for his performance in the 2008 season,

Houston is seeing its decision payoff in a large way.

Given all he's been through, Williams himself likely doubted he would ever be the draft's first pick. In fact, a family tragedy nearly ended his football career before it ever really began. When his brother-in-law, Marine Sgt. Nicolas Hodson, was killed in action in Iraq, Williams wanted to quit playing football in favor of getting a job to support his sister and her three suddenly fatherless young children. However, his older sister convinced Williams to return to school and he began to get noticed for his play at N.C. State.

IN THE HUDDLE
Williams finished the 2007 season with a franchise-record 14 sacks; second best in the league.

Williams' play as a junior wasn't always up to snuff and he often found himself watching from the sidelines rather than playing. He responded well to the benching though, finishing the year with 14 sacks while getting his team to win five of its last six games and then win a bowl game 14–0 over South Florida on New Year's Eve. More confident at this point, Williams performed well at the NFL scouting combine and suddenly

he was under consideration for the top pick. When his agent was able to work out a contract with Houston, the Texans did not hesitate to pick Williams, who would be the anchor of a new 4–3 defensive alignment under coach Gary Kubiak.

Williams posted 4.5 sacks as a rookie, which is a fair total for most first-year players, but fell short of expectations for the No. 1 draft pick. He also sustained a painful injury to his right foot after he was stepped on. He did not look good in executing his duties as a pass-rusher in a variety of positions along the line and the critics howled loudly. Williams used the attacks as motivation and came back with a superb performance

in 2007 that saw him record 14 sacks, the second-highest mark in the NFL. He became a fixture on the right side of the defensive line and started to understand that he had the size, speed and strength to dominate. Williams made 10 of his sacks in the last six games of the year, even though the Texans could do no better than an 8–8 record.

The Texans were a young group of players who expected the 2008 season to be a playoff year and Williams certainly did his part by recording 12 sacks. His great play got him named as a starter for the Pro Bowl, but Houston disappointed overall with another 8–8 season. Williams seemed to

relax a little more and worried less about being a No. 1 draft choice. The more focused lineman had four multi-sack games during the 2008 season and had his best performance versus Jacksonville when he nailed the quarterback three times in a 30–17 win.

Houston continues to develop as a team, but must cut down on mistakes in order to achieve its first post-season berth in franchise history. Williams will keep improving and may soon remind everyone of another defensive end who went first overall to Buffalo and did pretty well. His name was Bruce Smith and he is now in the Pro Football Hall of Fame.

REGGIE BUSH — New Orleans Saints

STEPHEN GOSTKOWSKI — New England Patriots

SHANE LECHLER — Oakland Raiders

DARREN SPROLES — San Diego Chargers

ADAM VINATIERI — Indianapolis Colts

LEON WASHINGTON — New York Jets

SPECIAL TEAMS

NEW ORLEANS SAINTS
★ ★ ★
RUNNING BACK
25

REGGIE BUSH

When a running back like Reggie Bush is drafted second overall, he's expected to have a major impact every time he touches the ball. Things haven't always worked out that way for the 2005 Heisman

CAREER HIGHLIGHTS

- Tied the Saints single-game record for touchdowns in a game with four against the San Francisco 49ers on December 3, 2006.
- Set an NFL record for catches by a rookie running back (88) in 2006.
- Led the NFL with three punt returns for touchdowns in 2008.

Trophy winner, but he is still very young and has shown he can be a more versatile player than many expected when the New Orleans Saints selected him in 2006. When he gets into the open field, Bush can be one of the most dangerous players in the entire NFL — he just doesn't excel at taking a simple handoff and plunging into the line.

Bush had some moments of greatness during 2008, especially in two games against Minnesota and Oakland. He ripped those squads for 344 total yards while scoring a total of four touchdowns. It was interesting to note two of the scores came from punt returns, one on a pass, while the other major came on

a run from scrimmage. While the Saints lost to the Vikings, Bush tied an NFL record by returning two punts for TDs in the same game. He also set a club record for most punt return yards in one game with 176. It was one of the more memorable performances of the 2008 season, but not exactly the way most people thought Bush would make his mark in the league — that as a premier running back.

Bush worked hard at preparing himself to be more of an inside runner, but he is quickly finding out the Saints are more suited to getting him the ball away from traffic and letting him do his thing. The New Orleans offensive line is more adept at pass blocking and is still developing as a group. In just three seasons, Bush has already caught 213 passes — with eight TDs to his credit — and a good number of them were completions behind the line of scrimmage. His rushing totals are not so impressive, although his 3.8 yards per carry was up slightly from his previous seasons.

Bush may never develop into the franchise savoir many hoped he would become, but he is proving to be an effective player. His work on special teams as a return man could yet prove to be his ultimate weapon. The 6-foot, 203-pound runner needs to stay healthy and if Bush keeps getting the ball in the right spots, he'll always have a chance to leave a big impression.

STEPHEN GOSTKOWSKI

The fantasy of playing Major League Baseball still hasn't quite left Stephen Gostkowski. He'd love the opportunity to be on the mound at Boston's Fenway Park, giving one the impression he'd be just as comfortable there as he is booting field goals in the NFL.

By his own admission, Gostkowski owes his football career to life on the diamond. He dominated as an overpowering right-handed pitcher at Madison (Mississippi) Central High School and earned a baseball scholarship to Memphis, even though he was also an all-state honoree in football and soccer.

Gostkowski realized after his freshman year that football afforded him his best shot at pro sports, so he became a walk-on to the Memphis football program. By the time his college career was over, he'd set a new school record with 369 points.

In 2006, the New England Patriots faced a kicking problem as the ever-popular Adam Vinatieri was a free agent. That year, the Pats picked Gostkowski 118th overall in the draft, making him one of two kickers selected that year as Virginia's Kurt Smith went 188th overall to San Diego.

By the time the season rolled along, Gostkowski had unseated veteran Martin Gramatica for the kicking job in New England and became the only rookie kicker to debut with an NFL club that year,

finishing with 103 points.

Gostkowski's strong leg has served him and the Patriots well. While extra points were the order of the day through his first two seasons — Gostkowski set the NFL record with the most point-after attempts (74) and successes (also 74) in 2007 — by 2008 he was being called upon more frequently in field goal situations.

He finished 2008 with a club-record and NFL-leading 148 points — surpassing by seven Vinatieri's club mark set in 2004. Gostkowski's 36 field goals on 40 attempts in 2008 also eclipsed another regular season record for the Pats, that belonging to Tony Franklin, who booted 32 field goals in 1986.

Gostkowski set a career high with 17 points (four field goals, five extra points) in New England's 47–7 blowout of Super Bowl-bound Arizona during Week 16 of 2008.

The All-Pro voters certainly were impressed with Gostkowski's performance, granting him 28 of a possible 50 votes as he easily outdistanced 44-year-old John Carney of the New York Giants. Gostkowski, only 24 at the time, also picked up his first Pro Bowl selection thanks to a poll of NFL players and coaches. There is no question his leg will put him in line for many more honors in the years to come.

CAREER HIGHLIGHTS

- Ranks fifth in active kickers with 85.5 percent field goal percentage.
- Has only missed one extra point in 158 attempts over three seasons.
- Kicked the longest field goal in Patriots playoff history when he connected on a 50-yard boot at San Diego on January 14, 2007.

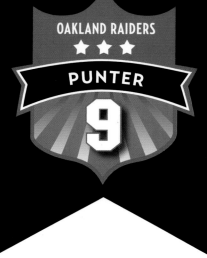

SHANE LECHLER

CAREER HIGHLIGHTS

• Has led the NFL in punting yards twice; 2003 and 2008.

• Had at least one punt of 50 yards or more in 33 consecutive games from Week 13 of 2003 through Week 14 of 2005, the longest streak by any player since the AFL-NFL Merger in 1970.

Punter Shane Lechler can do it all. He can boot it long — which is his trademark; he can boot it with plenty of hang time on it and he can even air it out effectively against the elements. He can also bury opponents in the coffin corner, that crucial piece of real estate just before — but not in — the endzone.

Born in East Bernard, Texas, Lechler comes from an athletic family. His father played football at Baylor while his mother played basketball there. Lechler and his brother eventually punted for Texas A&M. In fact, Lechler's wife was an all-American volleyball player with the Aggies.

Lechler lettered in football, baseball and basketball at East Bernard High before heading to college and firmly establishing himself as one of the NCAA's best-ever punters. He left the Aggies with the NCAA's all-time records for average yards per punt (44.7) and most games with a 40-plus yard average (37). In 1998, the Aggies benefited from Lechler's amazing 21 coffin corners and he added 17 such opponent-deflating kicks as a senior.

Only one punter was selected in the 2000 NFL draft: Lechler, in the fifth round by the Oakland Raiders (142nd overall). Since then, the kicking game for the Raiders has been the domain of Lechler (punting) and Sebastian Janikowski (place kicking).

Lechler's accomplishments rank among the NFL's all-time best. Through 2008, his 46.8-yard punting average ranked No. 1 in NFL annals, rising past the 45.1-yard average belonging to the fabled Sammy Baugh. Lechler's 49.1-yard average in 2007 is the best in Raiders history.

Consistency is the true measure of just how effective Lechler has been. In his first pro season, his 45.91 average just missed equaling the NFL rookie record of 45.92 set by Detroit's Frank Sinkwich in 1943. Through his first nine NFL campaigns, Lechler's season average dipped below 45.7 yards only once, in 2002 when he averaged 42.5 yards on a career-low 53 punts. By the end of 2008 Lechler had racked up six All-Pro selections and four Pro Bowl honors.

When Lechler arrived on the Raiders scene, his punting contributed to seasons that produced records of 12–4, 10–6 and 11–5, with Oakland reaching the post-season on every occasion. That peaked in his third year, when the Raiders reached Super Bowl XXXVII before losing 48–21 to Tampa Bay.

The Raiders then went into a freefall, but the same couldn't be said for Lechler. With every passing season and despite the overall performance of his club, his majestic boots remain a highlight for the Raiders and the league.

DARREN SPROLES

SAN DIEGO CHARGERS
★ ★ ★
RETURN SPECIALIST
43

Checking into the world weighing 10 pounds, the nickname "Tank" was most appropriate for Darren Sproles. Now, despite Sproles' stature of 5-foot-6 and 181 pounds, the Tank name has stuck, and there is no doubt he has earned the name he never grew into — a mighty good thing if San Diego happens to be your favorite NFL team.

With 23 school records to his credit, a strong case could be made Sproles is the best football player ever to come out of Kansas State. Selected by the Chargers in the fourth round (130th overall) in 2005, Sproles has been a vital element for San Diego, although less heralded than running backs LaDainian Tomlinson and, for a time, Michael Turner.

However, when Tomlinson was felled by injuries, Sproles entered the picture in spectacular fashion. The Indianapolis Colts will attest to that as their inability to halt Sproles during playoff games in 2007 and 2008 factored into painstaking losses.

In the second round of the 2007 playoffs, the Chargers unseated the defending Super Bowl-champion Colts at Indianapolis, 28–24. Sproles scored a 56-yard TD on a strike from quarterback Philip Rivers in the third quarter to put the Chargers up 21–17.

A year later, in the post-season's first round, Sproles totaled 328 all-purpose yards: he rushed for 105 yards and two TDs, returned kicks and punts for 178 yards and caught five passes for 45 yards. He touched off wild celebrations in San Diego when he romped to the 22-yard TD that gave the Chargers the win, 23–17 in overtime.

During the 2008 regular season, Sproles generated an electrifying 2,297 all-purpose yards: 1,376 on kick returns, 249 on punt returns, 342 on receptions and 330 rushing. That was well up from 2007 when he netted 1,432 yards in a comeback season after missing all of 2006 with a broken ankle. Sproles turned in his best season returning kicks as a rookie in 2005 with 1,528 of his 1,696 all-purpose yards compiled running back kicks.

Before becoming a Charger, he fulfilled the wishes of his late mother (who passed away of cancer in April 2004) by forgoing an early opportunity at the NFL draft and returning to Kansas State to complete his degree in speech pathology. Sproles has lived with a speech impediment and he's constantly worked to curtail his stuttering problem.

Of course, his play on the field speaks for itself.

CAREER HIGHLIGHTS

- Ranked second in the NFL with 2,297 all-purpose yards in 2008.
- His 1,376 kick return yards was ranked third in 2008.
- His 13.9 yards per touch ranked fourth in 2008.

INDIANAPOLIS COLTS
★ ★ ★
KICKER
4

ADAM
VINATIERI

A dam Vinatieri does his best work when he's making a kick with the game on the line. Such was the case when the Indianapolis Colts hosted the New England Patriots on November 2, 2008. The 36-year-old stepped up and drilled a 52-yard field goal to give the Colts a much-needed 18–15 win over the rival Pats — Vinatieri's original NFL club. The Colts had no doubt their kicker was money in the bank when they sent him out onto the field to win the game. Former Indy coach Tony Dungy had watched Vinatieri bang kicks through from 55 yards out in the pre-game warmup, so he was very confident a 52-yard attempt was essentially a sure thing.

Vinatieri's heroics in the 2008 season were not over after knocking off his former club. On November 23, he kicked his 22nd career game-winning field goal (a kick made in the last minute of the fourth quarter or overtime) during a 23–20 win over the San Diego Chargers. This time it was a 51-yard attempt that kept the Colts' playoff hopes alive as the clock ticked off the final seconds of the game. It was sweet for Vinatieri to nail the long kick against the Chargers because a year earlier he missed a very makeable 29-yard attempt that allowed San Diego to hang onto a 23–21 win. No one on the Colts doubted their kicker would be able to come back and

make the kind of kick that forged a reputation for Vinatieri as "Mr. Clutch."

A native of Yankton, South Dakota, Vinatieri joined the Patriots as a free agent after playing for the Amsterdam Admirals of the World Football League. The 1996 season saw the 6-foot-2, 202-pound kicker record 120 points for New England and he has never looked back. He has recorded no fewer than 100 points in all of his 12 NFL seasons to date and has participated in five Super Bowls, winning four times. His first Super Bowl win, in 2002, is still the most memorable as he kicked a 48-yarder on the last play of the game to help the Patriots knock off the heavily favored St. Louis Rams 17–14. Two seasons later his 41-yard kick with four seconds to play got the Patriots passed Carolina 32–29 in the Super Bowl, while a 22-yard kick sealed a 24–21 win by New England over Philadelphia in Super Bowl XXXIX. Super Bowl XLI saw him record three field goals and the Colts beat Chicago 29–17, ensuring Indianapolis was happy it had signed Vinatieri away from the Pats as a free agent in 2006.

If he is able to stay healthy, there may be no limit to the records and Super Bowl rings Vinatieri will own before he retires.

CAREER HIGHLIGHTS

- Holds NFL career post-season records with 42 field goals, 51 attempts, 177 points and 23 consecutive games scoring.
- Tied for most field goals made in post-season game with five versus Indianapolis on January 18, 2004.
- Only player in NFL history to record successful field goals in four Super Bowls.

LEON WASHINGTON

NEW YORK JETS
★ ★ ★
RETURN SPECIALIST
29

When Leon Washington blazed his way through the coverage of the New England Patriots for a 92-yard kick return TD during Week 11 of 2008, the score was significant. It was in an exciting contest that renewed a bitter rivalry between the Pats and the Jets — a contest won 34–31 by the Jets in overtime at Foxborough. It was also the game in which Washington produced his fourth career kickoff return TD, a club record.

"Neon" Leon had already put up a franchise record in 2007 with three kickoff return scores in one season. That placed him in a group of 12 returners who'd accomplished that thrilling feat. That year, Washington averaged 27.5 yards per kickoff return, churning out 1,291 yards on 47 returns. He was also the recipient of the Jets internal Curtis Martin MVP Award.

Washington's numbers for 2008 were just about equal to the numbers of his stellar 2007 campaign: 48 kickoff returns, 1,231 yards and an average of 25.6. Naturally, his contributions were in multi-roles. In 2008, his 29 punt returns and 303 PR yards were personal bests; he rushed the ball 76 times for 448 yards and established career highs in pass receiving with 47 catches, 355 yards and his first two TDs through the air.

Washington claimed 19 votes to edge out (by three) Tampa Bay's Clifton Smith for the AP All-Pro spot at kick returner. It was Washington's first such honor as was his selection to the AFC's Pro Bowl squad.

The Florida State product was selected by the Jets in the fourth round of the 2006 NFL Draft. The Jets gained that pick from the Kansas City Chiefs for the signing of Jets head coach Herm Edwards. Coincidentally, the kicker Washington beat for his 92-yard romp against New England was Stephen Gostkowski, the player selected right after Washington.

Washington came out of the Bobby Bowden factory with the Seminoles and did something for the college football coaching icon that no one else has done: score a TD in five different ways (kick return, punt return, rushing, receiving and fumble return).

Despite his college credentials, by the time Washington arrived on the NFL scene, Jets head coach Eric Mangini considered him lacking in playing shape and unable to hold onto the ball. Washington believes Mangini's tough love approach proved beneficial in his evolution in the pro ranks. But what coaches and teammates have discovered about Washington is his thorough preparation. He is a devoted film watcher, scouring tendencies of opponents on return coverage. His talent, speed and agility combined with his attention to detail have made him one of the game's most feared returners.

CAREER HIGHLIGHTS

- His three kick returns for TDs led the NFL in 2007.
- Posted 2,337 all-purpose yards in 2008 to lead the NFL.
- Selected to the 2008 Pro Bowl.

LINEBACKERS

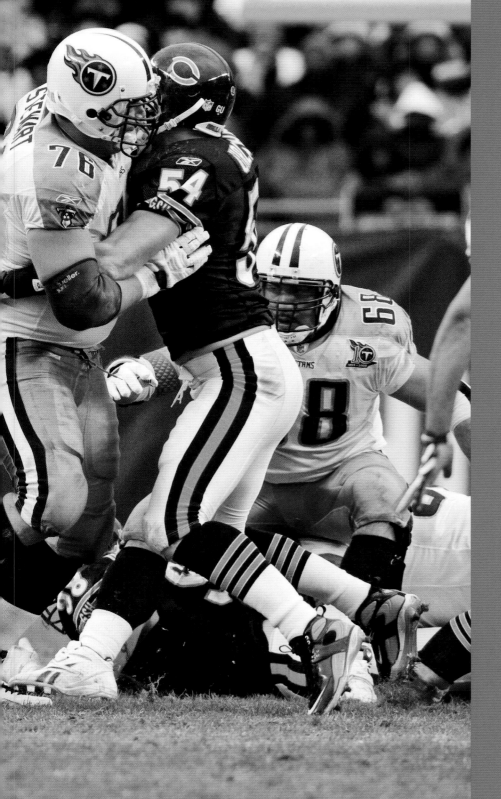

LANCE BRIGGS — Chicago Bears

JAMES FARRIOR — Pittsburgh Steelers

JAMES HARRISON — Pittsburgh Steelers

RAY LEWIS — Baltimore Ravens

JOEY PORTER — Miami Dolphins

DEMARCUS WARE — Dallas Cowboys

PATRICK WILLIS — San Francisco 49ers

LANCE BRIGGS

CHICAGO BEARS
★ ★ ★
LINEBACKER
55

His approach is predicated on two things: playing football and making money. No one can dispute Lance Briggs' value as the weak-side linebacker for the Chicago Bears. But at various times in his first six seasons with the Bears, his off-field bravado has overtaken his on-field accomplishments.

Briggs views himself as a football player and as his own chief executive officer, and it's important to look after No. 1 when it comes to contract demands. He's disowned the Chicago Bears and threatened to have played his last game for the franchise on more than one occasion, and has even termed his chances of returning to the Windy City as "slim at best" during one spin at free agency.

But each time, when all was said and done, No. 55 was back with the Bears. From the club's viewpoint, the Bears openly admitted talking trade with other clubs for the 6-foot-1, 240-pounder, but they never quite got what they wanted. So, they remained together.

IN THE HUDDLE
Briggs is third in team history, behind Mike Brown and Bennie McRae, with three career interceptions returned for touchdowns; Brown and McRae have four.

Born in Los Angeles and raised in Sacramento, Briggs thought there was a chance he'd end up in California, signing with the San Francisco 49ers after the 2007 season. The only problem was when those negotiations were going on, Briggs was under contract to the Bears and San Francisco was penalized for tampering.

The fine? San Francisco swapped its third round draft position in 2008 (70th) for Chicago's third round spot (75th) and the 49ers also forfeited their fifth round pick. Meanwhile Briggs, who had been tabbed the Bears' franchise player in 2007, eventually inked a six-year, $36-million deal with the Bears in March 2008.

Briggs came out of Elk Grove High School in Sacramento,

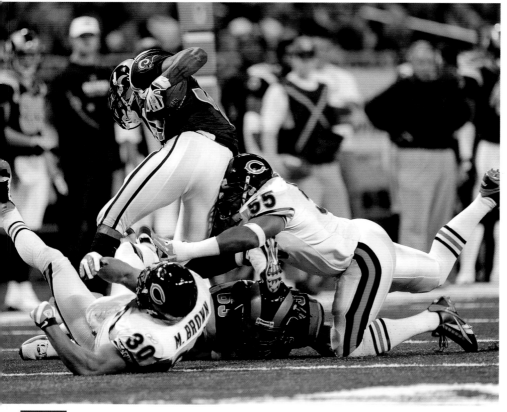

where he excelled in football and track. His 308 tackles (205 solo) with the University of Arizona Wildcats make it easy to understand why he was a three-time first-team All-Pac 10 linebacker.

The Bears added Briggs in the third round (68th overall) of the 2003 NFL draft. Briggs claimed a roster spot that year and moved up from reserve to starter in his fourth NFL game. He has the distinction of becoming the first NFL player to return the first three interceptions of his pro career for touchdowns, a feat he accomplished from 2003–2005.

Briggs earned his fourth consecutive trip to Hawaii in 2008, and for the fifth consecutive season he checked in with more than 100 tackles, finishing 24th in the league and tops on the Bears with 110. His career best was 130 in 2006 when Brian Ulracher paced the Bears in takedowns with 141.

Urlacher and Briggs became the heart of the Bears defense in 2006, with each jockeying for leadership in tackles and eventually propelling Chicago into Super Bowl XLI, a 29–17 loss to Indianapolis. That off-season, right after Chicago had dubbed him its franchise player,

Briggs made news: in August of 2007, he was involved in an automobile mishap, crashing his Lamborghini and leaving the scene of the accident on a Chicago expressway. Pleading guilty, he was fined less than $500 and given 120 hours of community service.

The 2006 Bears went 13–3 en route to the Super Bowl, but slipped to a disappointing 7–9 in 2007 and improved marginally to 9–7 in 2008. The defense that surrendered just 255 points in 2006 hasn't been as ferocious since, yielding 348 and 350 points in the two ensuing years.

When they reached Super Bowl XLI, Chicago's defense was fifth in the NFL, but in 2008 had dropped to a tie for 16th. The "Monsters of the Midway" simply lost some of their bite.

Urlacher has hit the big 3–0 in terms of age and the Bears mainstay up the middle will have to prove detractors wrong and show once more he's still effective. Briggs, who's two years younger than Urlacher, and signed through 2013, continues as one of the NFL's best outside linebackers. He's out to make it his business getting the Bears back into the post-season.

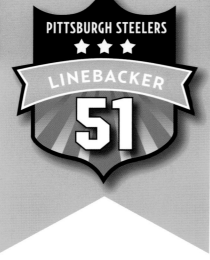

PITTSBURGH STEELERS
LINEBACKER
51

JAMES FARRIOR

Happy Days could very well be the working title of James Farrior's career with the Pittsburgh Steelers. He does have a connection to the popular TV show that ran from 1974 to 1984 because his parents nicknamed him "Potsie" after the character played by Anson Williams.

Why? Well, it seems Farrior, born in 1975, developed a potbelly, hence, the affectionate reference as Potsie. His Steeler teammates still refer to the popular inside linebacker that way. However, they do so respectfully, knowing the perennial leader among Steelers tacklers has quietly become one of the game's finest linebackers and is one of the team's captains.

Farrior is the consummate team player and committed to the Steelers. When he negotiated his five-year, $18.5-million contract extension in August of 2008, he made it clear to his agent he wanted to end his career as a Steeler and was willing to accept any role the club envisioned. That included accepting less playing time to accommodate the development of younger players.

Instead, Farrior once again led the Steelers in tackles (with 133) and earned his second career Pro Bowl selection while finishing fourth in voting at inside linebacker for the All-Pro team. The Steelers defense, under the direction of 71-year-old coordinator Dick LeBeau, allowed the fewest points per game in the NFL at 13.9 and the fewest yards with just 237.2 per game.

Farrior made 11 or more tackles in seven of 16 games in 2008, then had nine apiece during playoff wins over San Diego and Baltimore to lead the Steelers each time. In Super Bowl XLIII, Farrior topped the Steelers again with seven tackles (six of them solo) and although the Arizona Cardinals had more success penetrating the Steelers defense than most did this season, Pittsburgh still forced some key turnovers in the franchise's unprecedented sixth championship.

Born in Ettrick, Virginia, Farrior was a three-sport star (football, track and basketball) at Matoaca High School. His red No. 89 jersey hangs on Matoaca's Wall of Fame. He was a standout in college with the Virginia Cavaliers and a first round selection of Bill Parcells and the New York Jets in 1997.

___

IN THE HUDDLE
Led the Pittsburgh Steelers in 2008 with 133 total tackles.

___

Playing the outside spot in the Jets' defensive scheme, Farrior never made the explosive impact envisioned when he was drafted eighth overall. Despite racking up a career-high 142 tackles in 2001, the Jets parted ways with Farrior in a move they would come to regret. Unwanted in such places as Buffalo and Cleveland, Farrior's Pittsburgh-based agent got him a shot with the Steelers.

Moved to inside linebacker, where he would eventually form a partnership with Larry Foote, Farrior was instantly at home. Now,

CAREER HIGHLIGHTS

- Two-time Pro Bowl selection (2004, 2008).

- Drafted eighth overall from the University of Virginia by the New York Jets in 1997.

- Recorded a career-high six sacks in 2007.

- Finished second on the team in quarterback pressures in 2007.

- Led the Steelers in tackles for the last three seasons (2006–2008).

No. 51 is a permanent fixture, maintaining the Steelers tradition of employing steel-tough linebackers such as Andy Russell, Jack Ham, Jack Lambert, Greg Lloyd, Levon Kirkland and Joey Porter. In his first seven seasons with the Steelers, Farrior recorded 119 or more tackles four times, including 141 in 2003. He had a career-high four interceptions and 113 interception-return yards in 2004.

Farrior also gained a Pro Bowl selection in 2004, when he finished behind Baltimore free safety Ed Reed for the NFL defensive player of the year award. A steady player chiseled out of the Steeler tradition, his lunch-bucket approach over the long term contributes to making his club a better team. Farrior doesn't go out of his way to be flashy or blow his own horn, nor does he resent other linebackers gaining individual honors ahead of him.

He's grateful to be a two-time Super Bowl winner, but intends on adding to his ring collection. The victory in Super Bowl XLIII did fulfill one of his desires; he wanted the Steelers to be the first team U.S. president Barack Obama welcomed to the White House.

Given Obama's campaign was endorsed by some Steeler heavyweights, he was rooting for Pittsburgh. The exciting win over Arizona made for one mighty happy day for Farrior, the Steelers and the new chief at the White House.

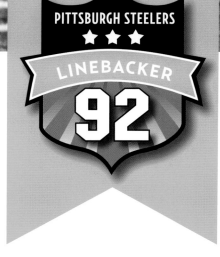

PITTSBURGH STEELERS
LINEBACKER 92

JAMES HARRISON

CAREER HIGHLIGHTS

- NFL defensive player of the year 2008.

- Two-time Pro Bowl selection (2007, 2008).

- Lead the Steelers to the top-ranked defense in the NFL in 2008.

- Recorded a career-high 16 sacks in 2008; his previous best was 8.5.

Pittsburgh linebacker James Harrison might be about the last person anyone would select as the player who would set a Super Bowl record for the longest play in the history of the championship game. However that is exactly what happened when the Steelers beat the Arizona Cardinals 27–23 in Super Bowl XLIII.

Late in the second quarter with the Cardinals about to take the lead, Arizona quarterback Kurt Warner dropped back to complete a short pass from Pittsburgh's two-yard line. Harrison looked like he was going to blitz from his linebacker position, but quickly took a step back and snared Warner's pass. He then began an improbable, rambling, somewhat stumbling run that took him 100 yards for a Pittsburgh touchdown as the clock ran out to end the first half.

Harrison used his teammates' blocks wisely as he tight-roped down the sideline and managed to avoid potential tacklers until just before the endzone. The exhausted Harrison collapsed, taking a double hit as he crossed the goal line, but hung on to the ball. Instead of being down 14–10, the Steelers were now up 17–7. There was no doubt it was a key moment in the contest and kept the momentum on Pittsburgh's side. The Steelers

eventually needed a last-minute drive to seal the victory.

It was a big surprise Harrison was on the field, let alone making one of the most memorable plays in the history of football's greatest spectacle. Harrison was born in Akron, Ohio, and attended Kent State, but was never drafted by an NFL team. The Steelers signed Harrison as a free agent in 2002, but he was only able to make the practice roster and played just one game that year. Most of the next year was the same story and that got him released in 2003. He also tried out for the Baltimore Ravens, but was released. They suggested Harrison try NFL Europe, a lead that went nowhere.

IN THE HUDDLE
Harrison signed a $51.75-million, six-year contract ($20 million is guaranteed) after the Steelers Super Bowl XLIII win that will make him the second highest-paid player in franchise history.

The 6-foot, 240-pound linebacker thought about quitting and taking up a career as a bus driver. However, Steelers coach Bill Cowher was able to talk him into returning for another try. By his own admission, Harrison was very stubborn in his first go with Pittsburgh. Added maturity helped

grant him a little bit of an opportunity when an injury opened up a spot on the special teams squad. He knew it was his last chance and made the most of it, even though it took him some time to crack the starting lineup. Harrison was not a starter when the Steelers beat Seattle in Super Bowl XL, but the victory gave him a taste of what it's like to be on a winning team.

When Pittsburgh released linebacker Joey Porter in 2007, it opened a starting spot for Harrison. He played in all 16 games and was named the team MVP, while also earning a Pro Bowl start. The 31-year-old really started to blossom during the 2008 season, beginning the year in great style with three sacks in the opening game against the Houston Texans during a 38–17 Steelers victory. He was named the NFL's defensive player of the year and was the unquestioned leader of the best defense in all of football.

Harrison showed a hunger to be the best and was pretty much able to do as he pleased within defensive coordinator Dick Lebeau's 3–4 scheme. Although he is not tall, Harrison is able to use his low center as leverage against bigger offensive linemen. He has great speed, strength and a nose for the quarterback, recording 16 sacks and forcing seven fumbles in 2008.

Harrison is driven by the fact he must prove himself — a trait he developed after being released so many times — and does not like to hear accolades about his play. But now that he has helped a team to a Super Bowl win he may start hearing comparisons to former great Steeler linebackers like Jack Lambert and Jack Ham. It might be a bit early to say Harrison is similar to Pittsburgh's gridiron legends, but there is no doubt he has become a part of Pittsburgh's proud football legacy.

BALTIMORE RAVENS
★ ★ ★

LINEBACKER
52

RAY LEWIS

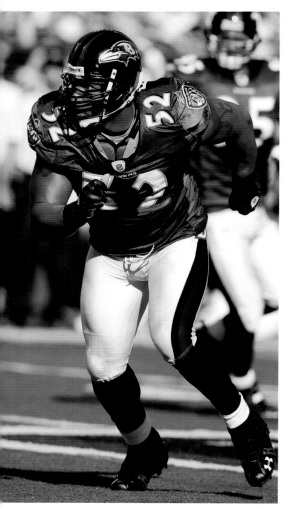

M iddle linebacker Ray Lewis is as ferocious a player at the age of 33 as he was the day the Baltimore Ravens selected him 26th overall in the 1996 NFL draft. No player and team in the NFL are as intrinsically tied as Lewis and Baltimore. He leads in a very loud and proud manner, making his teammates accountable to him. The way he whips up his team prior to games is equally fun and scary to watch. Yet Lewis' fellow Ravens react well to his antics and it is easy to see that the leader of the punishing Raven defense has his teammates attention and total respect.

None of what Lewis preaches would work if he weren't such an on-field leader. He actually takes attempts to score against the Ravens personally, and incites the same approach in others. Early in the 2008 season when the Ravens were playing archrival Pittsburgh, Lewis obliterated Steelers rookie running back Rashard Mendenhall with a tackle so crushing it broke Mendehall's shoulder and put him out for the season. During one game against the Houston Texans, Lewis made nine tackles on his own and two interceptions, retuning them for 43 total yards.

In the 2008 playoffs, he hit Tennessee running back Ahmard Hall with such force he knocked off the running back's helmet. The hit seemed to deflate the Titans — as did Baltimore's pounding attacks on Tennessee star runner Chris Johnson — and the Ravens went on to win the contest 13–10 and got themselves back to the AFC championship game. They lost that contest to the Steelers, but it was through no fault of the Baltimore defense.

Lewis has been able to stay on top by committing himself to a fitness program that keeps his 6-foot-1, 250-pound body in tip-top shape all year round. If aging has had any effect on Lewis, he more than makes up for it with a tremendous work ethic and a determination that keeps him about ten years younger than he is.

IN THE HUDDLE
Lewis was twice named the NFL's defensive player of the year (2000 and 2003).

He has also become more of a student of the game and enjoys the hours he puts in watching film. Other Raven players take their cue from Lewis and join the linebacker for his sessions studying the opposition. Lewis believes the more he studies opponents, the easier the games become.

When he first joined the NFL, Lewis looked up to the likes of former Baltimore stars Rod Woodson and Shannon Sharpe as they passed on their wisdom to him. Now it is Lewis giving lessons to his younger mates. He loves to see the Ravens defense attack a ball carrier and make the runner pay a physical price — just like he's relished doing for years.

As much as Lewis is intimidating to both teammates and opponents, he foolishly landed himself in trouble that might have put him in prison for life in 2000. While Lewis was able to escape a murder charge by providing testimony against the other accused persons and by pleading guilty to a lesser charge of obstruction of justice, it appeared his off-field reputation was permanently damaged. He served one year of probation and was fined $250,000 by the NFL. Since, he has quietly worked for various charitable causes and has managed to steer clear of trouble. He may never be seen as a complete role model, but Lewis can say he has reformed his life off the field.

On the field, Lewis has now completed 13 NFL seasons and has recorded 1,254 tackles, by far a team record. He has 28 career interceptions to go along with 33.5 career sacks. He has earned numerous awards during his illustrious career, none bigger than being named MVP of Super Bowl XXXV when the Ravens whipped the New York Giants 34–7. As of 2008, Lewis and kicker Matt Stover were the only remaining players from that championship team still with Baltimore. He has also been named defensive player of the year and is a perennial member of the Pro Bowl team. The only thing left for Lewis to accomplish is getting his team back to the Super Bowl and with his

CAREER HIGHLIGHTS

• 2000 NFL Super Bowl MVP.

• 10-time Pro Bowl Selection (1997–2001, 2003, 2004, 2006–2008).

• Led the NFL in tackles five times.

• Established a single-season franchise record for tackles in 2003 with 225.

leadership skills, nobody should bet against him.

In early March Baltimore signed Lewis to a seven-year deal which will allow him to retire a Raven. His incentive-laden deal also assures Lewis $10 million in the first year of the contract.

MIAMI DOLPHINS
★ ★ ★

LINEBACKER
55

JOEY PORTER

CAREER HIGHLIGHTS

- Only player to record at least five sacks in the last nine consecutive seasons (2000–2008).
- Led the Dolphins with 17.5 sacks in 2008 for a total of 96 yards in losses.
- Four-time Pro Bowl selection (2002, 2004, 2005, 2008).
- Drafted 73rd overall from Colorado State University by the Pittsburgh Steelers in 1999.

It was at least a bit surprising when the Pittsburgh Steelers released linebacker Joey Porter prior to the 2007 season, especially given he'd led them to a Super Bowl championship just a couple years before being let go. At the time of his dismissal, Porter had racked up 60 quarterback sacks in eight seasons with the Steelers. However, in the salary cap era, a $1-million payment for just being on a roster is very significant, as was the $4-million salary he would have earned in 2007. The good news for guys like Porter is there is no shortage of teams willing to sign talented players who get caught up in the numbers game. The Miami Dolphins quickly moved in and gave the All-Pro a five-year deal worth $32 million.

A team looking to re-build will often hand out a lucrative deal to get a player they desperately want. Sometimes it works out well and other times it turns out to be a waste of money.

Porter has been on both sides of the equation in just two years with the Dolphins. In 2007, coach Cam Cameron wanted new players to replace those who had gone 6–10 the year before. It did not work

out so well for the former San Diego Chargers assistant as the Dolphins recorded one of the worst years in NFL history with a 1–15 record. Needless to say Cameron was gone at the end of the season and Porter (who had recorded only 5.5 sacks) had to wonder whether signing with such a poor team was a good idea after all. However, longtime NFL coach Bill Parcells took over the management of Miami's football operations and named Dallas assistant Tony Sparano as the Dolphins' new head coach. Sparano saw two players as the key to the success for his team in 2008. One was a late acquisition in quarterback Chad Pennington from the New York Jets. The other was Porter, who was seen as the leader of the defense, especially with defensive end Jason Taylor having departed for Washington.

The hyper-aggressive linebacker seemed to relish his status on the team. Porter is loud, brash and can talk up the opposition like few others in the NFL. He may have unusual views and exceptional wit, but there is little doubt that he can get inside the heads of the opposition and take them off their game. And the Dolphins don't seem to mind having such a mouthy player talking trash to others, even though Porter was fined $20,000 for his comments about a referee after the Dolphins lost to Houston. Sometimes Porter's talking starts before game day, or in the pre-game warm-ups when he lets the opponents know they're in for a long afternoon.

Once, Porter indicated that preparing for the Matt Cassel-led New England Patriots wasn't a difficult task. Porter then went out and sacked Cassel three times in a 38–13 win by the Dolphins. When Porter backs up his talk with first-rate performances like he did versus New England, opponents take notice and pay special attention to the hard-

hitting 6-foot-3, 255-pounder. Porter is often double teamed, but that just means other Dolphin defenders are able to make more tackles.

IN THE HUDDLE
Porter and Clay Mathews are the only players in NFL history to record at least 60 sacks and 10 interceptions in their career.

In 2008 Porter recorded an AFC-best 17.5 sacks — the second-best mark in the entire NFL and just one short of the team record held by the departed Taylor and Bill Stanfill — which helped the Dolphins make a remarkable turn around with an

11–5 record and an unlikely AFC East Division crown. No Miami fan could have predicted such an aboutface in 2008, especially with 30 new players on the roster. Porter brought a great deal of fire to the Miami defense and he was very good in the fourth quarter when many games were on the line. His end-of-game tackle against the San Francisco 49ers in week 15 of 2008 is a classic example of Porter making the plays needed to close out a tight, must-win contest. Porter was rewarded for his strong effort in 2008 with a selection as a starter in the 2008 Pro Bowl, and is now a mainstay with Miami.

DEMARCUS WARE

DALLAS COWBOYS
★ ★ ★
LINEBACKER
94

Removed from the grunts, groans and pain of the gridiron, Dallas Cowboy DeMarcus Ware is overjoyed every chance he has to hold his daughter, Marley. Ware and his wife, Taniqua, are high school sweethearts and they've always desired a big family. But after three failed pregnancies including the stillbirth of their son, Omar, the Wares adopted Marley as an infant. DeMarcus and Taniqua still envision a household with plenty of children some day.

Since February 2008, Marley has occupied much of their time and they've welcomed her with loving arms and openly discussed their family situation. The disclosure has been an eye-opener into the background of the overpowering player the Cowboys wanted when they made Ware their first choice (11th overall) in the 2005 NFL draft. His sack total alone indicates a steady climb: from 8.0 as a rookie in 2005 to a league-leading 20.0 in 2008. He set the Cowboys record for sacks in one season by a linebacker in 2007 with 14.0, and then proceeded to shatter it one year later.

Ware was born in Auburn, Alabama on July 31, 1982, and played football at Auburn High in his junior and senior years with Osi Umenyiora (who went on to the New York Giants) and Marcus Washington (who went on to the Washington Redskins) among his teammates. For Ware, participation in football was added to a sporting slate that also included the school's baseball, basketball and track squads. The opportunity to become a hometown hero at Auburn University never presented itself. Instead, he headed to Troy, Alabama and Troy University for one simple reason: it was the only suitor he had.

At Troy University, Ware concentrated more on maintaining his grades than football, so thoughts of reaching the NFL, while tantalizing, weren't top of mind for the business information systems graduate. When Ware completed his studies he became the first college grad in his family. The responsibility he showed in achieving his degree derives from his two inspirations — his mother and wife.

When not hitting the books, Ware was playing defensive end at Troy. He was a reserve as a freshman, but became a starter in the second game of his sophomore season, a year in which he posted 72 tackles, his career college high. Ware left Troy with the Sun Belt Player of the Year Award to go along with his hard earned degree.

The Cowboys were clearly trying to put some defense back in "Big D" when they used their first round pick to select Ware. He wasted no time accepting the load heaped on him, becoming only the second Cowboy rookie to tie or lead the team in sacks. Ware also became the first Cowboy to tie or lead the team in that category over his first four NFL seasons. Once told he

lacked the size and speed to thrive in football, Ware has completely defused that assessment. At 6-foot-4 and 262 pounds, he has remarkable ability as a pass rusher and a pass defender.

IN THE HUDDLE

In Ware's first four seasons he collected 53.5 sacks, nine more than all-time sacks leader Bruce Smith posted in his first four campaigns.

Ware posted sacks in the final three games of 2007 and the first seven contests of 2008. That tied the NFL mark of 10 consecutive games with a sack previously set by Denver's Simon Fletcher in 1992–93. Ware equaled the record with a three-sack performance at St. Louis

in Week 7, but it came during a stunning 34–14 loss to the Rams. It was a defeat that factored heavily in Dallas missing the playoffs in 2008 despite starting the season as one of the Super Bowl favorites.

While Ware's season was worthy of consideration as the NFL's defensive player of the year, he was disappointed when the honor went to Pittsburgh's James Harrison. The Steelers, with their sterling defense, made the post-season; Dallas didn't and many felt that weighed heavily with the voters, who gave Harrison 22 votes compared to 13 for Ware. Still, 2008 marked a third consecutive Pro Bowl honor for Ware and a third straight All-Pro nod (his second consecutive first-team selection). In the All-Pro poll, Ware

CAREER HIGHLIGHTS

- Three-time Pro Bowl selection (2006–2008).
- First player to win the Dick Butkus Award as the NFL's best linebacker.
- Is the first player in Cowboys history to lead or tie for the team lead in sacks his first four seasons with the team.

received 45 votes to Harrison's 38.

In 2008, the Dick Butkus Award — given annually to the top collegiate linebacker since 1985 — was expanded to include the pro and high school levels. Ware became the first NFL linebacker to be honored with the award.

PATRICK WILLIS

CAREER HIGHLIGHTS

- Two-time Pro Bowl Selection (2007, 2008).
- Was named the 49ers' defensive captain in 2008.
- Was the only rookie named to the All-Pro team in 2007.
- Set a franchise-record with 21 tackles in one game: 2007, Week 12 against Arizona.

Shortly after their final game of 2008, the San Francisco 49ers removed the "interim" tag from head coach Mike Singletary with a four-year pact aimed at righting the San Francisco ship. It was a move thoroughly endorsed by inside linebacker Patrick Willis, who, in his two NFL seasons, improved immeasurably under the tutorship of Singletary as a defense coach.

Singletary is one of the NFL's all-time gifted linebackers, earning his way to the Pro Football Hall of Fame thanks to a terrific career with the Chicago Bears from 1981 to 1992. Willis arrived on the NFL scene in 2007, garnering honors as NFL defensive rookie of the year to go along with All-Pro and Pro Bowl recognition.

The 49s closed 2008 with a 5–4 mark under Singletary, sparking hope the football gods might again shine on a once-proud organization that hasn't had much in the way of optimism since going 10–6 in 2002.

Willis is certainly a notable piece of the re-build. He arrived out of Ole Miss in spectacular fashion by leading the NFL with 174 tackles in 2007 before recording 141 in his sophomore season. Only Cleveland's D'Qwell Jackson (with 154) brought down more ball carriers in 2008.

At 6-foot-1 and 240 pounds, Willis has tremendous quickness and football instincts that flourish when he attacks head-on, drops back or goes sideline-to-sideline. In Week 2 of 2008, he returned his first NFL interception — at Seattle off Matt Hasselbeck — 86 yards for a TD. It was a momentum boost for the 49ers who surged back to score a 33–30 win.

IN THE HUDDLE

Willis set a San Francisco franchise record for the longest interception return by a linebacker with an 86-yard return in Week 2 of 2008.

Willis was selected 11th overall by the 49ers with their first of two first round draft picks in 2007. The team picked offensive tackle Joe Staley at the No. 28 position that year, a spot it obtained from New England.

Staley, Willis and Cleveland tackle Joe Thomas were the only rookies in 2007 to line up for every snap on their side of the ball. Any emergence by the 49ers in the years ahead will be linked back to draft day, 2007.

Born in Bruceton, Tennessee, on January 25, 1985, Willis lettered in football, basketball and baseball at Central High. Willis and his three siblings had a tough upbringing. After years of neglect by his biological father, his world changed

dramatically at the age of 16 when his basketball coach, Chris Finley, and Finley's wife, Julie, became his foster parents and guardians.

In 2006, Willis also endured the tragic loss of his 17-year-old brother, Detris, who drowned while swimming with friends. With constant support from the Finleys, Willis was able to maintain his solid perspective in life. As he studied liberal arts at Ole Miss, he capped a brilliant college career by finishing with 355 tackles over 45 games.

He captured the Dick Butkus Award as the outstanding collegiate linebacker in 2006, then gained defensive MVP honors for the South

Team at the 2007 Senior Bowl. Willis played his way into the 49ers starting lineup in 2007 with an awesome display of skill during the pre-season.

That relentless passion carried into the regular season, where Willis recorded 10-or-more tackles in 10 of his 16 games in 2007, including a 20-tackle performance against Tampa Bay in Week 16. Willis became the first defensive rookie for the 49ers to make first team All-Pro and the Pro Bowl since cornerback Ronnie Lott in 1981.

Willis had four games with 11-plus tackles in 2008, peaking with a season-high 18 against New

England in Week 5. Aspiring to one day be worthy of the Pro Football Hall of Fame like his mentor Singletary, Willis has counted such standouts as Ray Lewis, Terrell Owens, Emmitt Smith and Michael Irvin as players he's followed.

But now his drive is to establish his name while building a winning environment in the City by the Bay. Starting in 2009, the task of working with San Francisco's inside linebackers fell exclusively to Singletary's nephew, Vantz. There's no doubt Mike Singletary will still keep a close eye on Willis, too, because the head coach knows he's something special.

NNAMDI ASOMUGHA — Oakland Raiders

NICK COLLINS — Green Bay Packers

BRIAN DAWKINS — Denver Broncos

CORTLAND FINNEGAN — Tennessee Titans

TROY POLAMALU — Pittsburgh Steelers

ED REED — Baltimore Ravens

CHARLES WOODSON — Green Pay Packers

DEFENSIVE BACKS

NNAMDI ASOMUGHA

OAKLAND RAIDERS
★ ★ ★
CORNERBACK 21

The plight of the Oakland Raiders has created relatively little national coverage in recent years and that has deprived Nnamdi Asomugha of deserved exposure. He isn't a household name across football's massive expanse, but those who know the game realize this guy is good. Very good.

Some have already dubbed him the best cornerback in football, a crown he's wrestled away from Denver Bronco star Champ Bailey. And yet in 2008, Asomugha had just one interception. So how exceptional can he be?

The answer lies in the fact

opponents refuse to throw anywhere near him, figuring it can only lead to bad things. That keeps the ball a long way from his hands. It wasn't always so for Asomugha, of course, because when he arrived out of Cal-Berkley in 2003, the Raiders had Charles Woodson and Phillip Buchanon on the corners.

Asomugha filled in at several spots in the defensive backfield, making only one start in the 15 games he played at free safety. He also lived with the talk of some rivals wondering why the Raiders wasted their first round selection on him.

He started seven of 16

games in 2004, then got to play his natural position in 2005 by starting all 16 games at corner. His breakout season occurred in 2006 when he tied for third in the NFL with eight interceptions. One of his picks that season — off Pittsburgh's Ben Roethlisberger in Week 8 — was returned 24 yards for his first pro TD. It helped the Raiders upset the defending Super Bowl-champion Steelers 20–13 in what was the final win for Oakland in a miserable 2–14 season.

However, Asomugha had established his mark with Pro Bowl and All-Pro recognitions. His hard work had finally paid

CAREER HIGHLIGHTS

• Named to his first Pro Bowl in 2008.

• Led the Raiders in 2006 with 19 passes defended.

• Drafted 31st overall from the University of California by the Oakland Raiders in 2003.

• Set a University of California record in his senior year for the longest interception touchdown return (98 yards).

off and he gained the respect that eluded him initially. Suddenly, things got lonelier in his area. Even with the demands of man-on-man coverage, the rangy corner had opponents convinced passing against him wasn't worth it.

The Raiders put the franchise tag on Asomugha in 2008 and were expected to do the same for 2009. Working out a long-term deal with Asomugha would benefit all involved. In the process, it would keep an active member of the Bay Area in the community.

IN THE HUDDLE
Asomugha had a career-high eight interceptions in 2006, good for third in the NFL.

The 6-foot-2, 210-pound Asomugha was born in Lafayette, Louisiana. His parents, Godfrey (a petroleum engineer) and Lilian (a pharmacist), came from Nigeria to attend college in the U.S. Eventually, the Asomugha family settled in Los Angeles, where each of the four children learned the value of education.

Nnamdi, which means "Jesus Lives" in Nigerian, and his older brother, Chijioke, played Pop Warner football and other sports like basketball. That diversion became incredibly important in their lives with the sudden passing of their father when the boys were still teenagers.

Enamored with the playing style of former NFL stand out Deion Sanders, the Asomugha brothers went from stars at Nathaniel Narbonne High School in Los Angeles to the college gridiron. Chijioke joined Stanford while Nnamdi attended Cal. Of the two, Nnamdi was more heavily recruited, but the occasions they played each other proved to be a true test

of neutrality for their proud mother.

Since his early years, Nnamdi Asomugha showed a charitable side, even without being asked or prodded. So it comes as no surprise he's always given willingly to worthy causes, in Los Angeles, Berkley, Nigeria and now Oakland. Asomugha, who aspires to be a broadcaster once his playing days are over and already does some broadcasting work in the Bay Area, enjoys making appearances and offering inspiration to others.

He's received the Raiders

Commitment to Excellence Award for the player on the club who best exemplifies the "pride, poise and spirit" of the franchise. Given his track record, you can bet he'll continue to give back throughout his playing career and beyond.

In the meantime, Asomugha will carry on as one of the best — if not the premier — cover guy in the NFL. His lack of interceptions is deceptive, but he made Pro Bowl and All-Pro honors in 2008, so those who know this game realize there's an absolute gem on the corner for the Silver and Black.

GREEN BAY PACKERS
★ ★ ★
SAFETY
36

NICK COLLINS

CAREER HIGHLIGHTS

- Was second in the NFL with seven interceptions in 2008.
- Selected to first Pro Bowl in 2008.
- Was named the Packers' 2005 defensive rookie of the year.
- Drafted 51st overall from Bethune-Cookman University by the Green Bay Packers in 2005.

Some eyebrows were raised in 2005 when the Green Bay Packers used a second round draft choice obtained from New Orleans to select Bethune-Cookman defensive back Nick Collins. While he had the size and speed to be a free safety, the book on Collins was that he required time to develop.

The Packers had a gaping hole at safety because two-time All-Pro and Pro Bowler Darren Sharper was released the previous winter due to dollar differences. As it turned out, Sharper maintained his All-Pro and Pro Bowl status with the Minnesota Vikings, but the insertion of Collins into the Pack's defensive secondary also worked out.

Packers GM Ted Thompson was so confident in Collins that he bestowed jersey No. 36 on him. LeRoy Butler had previously worn that number in Green Bay and he was selected to the Pro Bowl on four occasions. Butler was assured the next member of the Pack to don his number would be a worthy candidate, further indicating Green Bay's belief in Collins. It also added some extra pressure on a young player entering the "Cheesehead" world of Packer Nation.

Collins got right into the mix, working with the Packers' first-team defense even before the team's first pre-season game. When he lined up for his NFL debut in 2005 he was the club's starting free safety, it stayed that way for the remaining 15 games of the season. Collins was the first rookie safety to launch a season with Green Bay since Chuck Cecil made the squad in 1988. He has been a stalwart ever since, occupying his spot on the field — and even playing the corner position from time to time when the defensive scheme calls for the dime package — for every game but three from 2005 through 2008. The only contests he missed were due to injury.

IN THE HUDDLE
Collins led the NFL with 295 interception return yards and three non-offensive touchdowns in 2008.

While at least one publication warned in its pre-season forecast that Collins might be in jeopardy of losing his job coming off a so-so 2007 campaign, he quelled such observations by showing he was still very much in control of things. His 2008 NFL season proved to be his most rewarding. Collins tied teammate Charles Woodson, Pittsburgh's Troy Polamalu and Tennessee's Michael Griffin for second in the NFL with seven interceptions. But Collins was the league leader with three picks returned for touchdowns and with

295 yards on interception returns. He also posted a career-high 84 tackles.

The Packers were knotted with the Titans and Chicago Bears for third place in interceptions during 2008, each with 22. Only Cleveland (23) and Baltimore (26) exceeded those totals. The Packers, largely because of Collins and company, were ahead of everyone in picks returned for TDs (6) and interception-return yards (685). Green Bay's backfield also allowed just 6.5 yards gained per pass, the sixth-lowest total in the NFL. Collins was rewarded in 2008 with his first Pro Bowl and All-Pro selections.

Gainesville, Florida, is the birthplace for Collins, but his

hometown is Cross City about 50 miles away. Given the speed he possesses now, it's not surprising that while attending Dixie County High School he was a quarterback, running back and defensive back in football, a guard in basketball and center fielder in baseball.

Under the NCAA's Proposition 48 guidelines, his lack of required academic score kept him out of football in his first year at Bethune-Cookman. But he made up for lost time. Collins went from a reserve linebacker in 2002 to safety over the next two years, where he made all-conference honors in 2003 and 2004. Of his 13 interceptions in college, he returned two for TDs.

His first TD as a pro and his first two-interception game in the NFL came at Chicago in the final game of 2006. He picked off a Rex Grossman toss intended for Desmond Clark and dashed for a 55-yard score in the first quarter, then snuffed out another Chicago possession by intercepting Brian Griese in the fourth quarter.

Collins has taken to community initiatives launched by the Packers. He's into bowling, action movies, fresh-water fishing and spending time with his wife and two young children. He's proven worthy of the decision to start him as a rookie and at just 25, Collins is a rare mix of youth and experience.

BRIAN DAWKINS

Philadelphia is a tough town and fans let their sporting heroes know when they are unhappy with their play. One exception to this rule was former Eagles safety Brian Dawkins, who was as beloved a player as you will have ever found in the City of Brotherly Love. An emotional leader with a fearless and inspiring style of play, Dawkins was the undisputed leader of the Eagles defense — one of the best units in the NFL in 2008. His strong desire to win is unquestioned and, at 36, Dawkins may be considered old by some, but his play during the 2008 season was good enough to earn him a five-year contract with Denver — making Dawkins 41 years old at its expiration.

IN THE HUDDLE

Dawkins became the first player in NFL history to record a sack, an interception, a fumble recovery and a touchdown reception in a single game when he did so against Houston in 2002.

The last few weeks of the Eagles' 2008 season were as emotional as any during Dawkins' 13 years in Philadelphia. First, the Eagles demolished the Dallas Cowboys (a team once favored to go to the Super Bowl) by a score of 44–6 to secure a playoff spot. Then, in its first playoff game, Philly defeated the Minnesota Vikings 26–14. Dawkins was a huge contributor to the win, sacking Vikings quarterback Tarvaris Jackson and making nine tackles overall. The Eagles followed up with another great defensive effort on the road and beat the defending Super Bowl champs, the New York Giants, by a 23–11 count, holding the home team to zero touchdowns. The Eagles missed out on a Super Bowl berth, losing to Arizona by a touchdown.

One year previous, the Eagles and Dawkins both looked like spent forces. The team finished 2007 8–8 while Dawkins had the worry of a trying pregnancy endured by his wife, Connie. The premature birth of twin daughters complicated life for Dawkins and his family, although there was a happy ending with everyone going home from the hospital in good condition. Dawkins registered only one interception all year long. Observers began to question the team and the normally reliable safety like never before. There were whispers Dawkins' play was declining considerably with age, but that is a natural reaction when players get older. The 2008 season also appeared to be going nowhere when the team was a mediocre 5–5–1, but Philadelphia suddenly re-grouped and found itself just one win away from the Super Bowl. Dawkins took the challenges to his abilities in stride

and even acknowledged that some of the talk might be true. However, he believed he had plenty to offer the team and then went out and showed he was very worthy of a Pro Bowl nomination as a reserve. He was also nominated for the Walter Payton Man of the Year Award, which recognizes a players' contribution to his community as well as his on-field performance.

Dawkins began his career with Philadelphia after the Eagles selected him 61st overall in the 1996 NFL draft. The 6-foot-2, 210-pound Dawkins was taken after a great career at Clemson University and he stepped into the Eagles lineup by starting 13 games as a rookie. He holds many Eagle records, including most career games played with 183. He's tied for most career interceptions (34)

and most selections to the Pro Bowl with seven. Dawkins shares some of these marks with legendary Eagle players like Chuck Bednarik, Reggie White, Eric Allen and Bill Bradley. He has also won 109 total games while a member of the Eagles — including 10 post-season wins — but one victory has proved to be elusive. Dawkins has only had one opportunity to play in the Super Bowl and the Eagles lost that 2005 contest 24–21 to the New England Patriots. The team has played in five NFC championship games during his time as an Eagle — a remarkable accomplishment in its own right.

As popular as Dawkins is with the Philadelphia fans, the team had to make a difficult decision as to whether they should bring him back or go with a younger player. Despite his great play in 2008, the

CAREER HIGHLIGHTS

- Collected his 34th career interception in 2008 to tie him with Bill Bradley and Eric Allen for the Eagles record.
- Seven-time Pro Bowl selection (1999, 2001, 2002, 2004–2006, 2008).
- Dawkins, Leroy Butler, Rodney Harrison, Ronde Barber are the only players in NFL history, to post at least 32 interceptions and 18 sacks.

Eagles decided to go with youth, and left Dawkins free to sign with the Denver Broncos, who ponied up $17 million to obtain the services of the 36-year-old. Dawkins' play in 2009 will determine which team made the better choice.

CORTLAND FINNEGAN

Cortland Finnegan expects game officials and the NFL league office to keep close tabs on him. His honesty in those matters fits right in with his character. Finnegan is feisty, loves to hit, gets mask-to-mask with opponents and backs up all his choice words with standout play. The right corner for the Tennessee Titans was fined numerous times by the NFL in 2008 as his rough play had game officials at the ready, hand-on-flag. Finnegan didn't cry that he was a marked man, but rather, said fines were okay with him because he knew the money would go to charity anyway.

In 2008, Finnegan made Pro Bowl and All-Pro selections, confirming what he provides to the Titans and their fans is a passion directed at winning. And victories were plentiful for the Titans in 2008, with the defense spearheading the club's 10–0 start and league-best 13–3 record.

Their ouster in the playoffs to their bitter rivals, the Baltimore Ravens, had nothing to do with the defense collapsing, but rather turnovers that kept curtailing potential scoring drives. The Tennessee defense, which was right at the bottom of the NFL in yards surrendered per game in 2006, improved to fifth in 2007 and was seventh in 2008.

The Titans also improved as ball-hawkers, seeing their number of interceptions go from 17 in 2006 to 20 in 2008. Free safety Michael Griffin paced the Titans in 2008 with seven picks, while Finnegan followed with five.

IN THE HUDDLE
Finnegan was the first person to be drafted from Samford University since Gary Fleming in 1969.

The aggression Finnegan brings to the Titans played a part in that turnaround. His rising stock in just two seasons resulted in the Titans extending his contract in the summer of 2008 with a four-year pact worth $17 million, including a $6-million signing bonus.

Not bad for a seventh round, 215th overall long shot out of — get this — the Samford University Bulldogs in Birmingham, Alabama. Finnegan, who some say is generously listed at 5-foot-10 and 188 pounds, is thriving in the underdog role. He's taken the challenge and responded with a fearless, tough and smart approach. He knows exactly what he's doing on the field and he's wise enough to realize he has a responsibility to the community off the field.

His sports hero was running back Barry Sanders, the offensive

CAREER HIGHLIGHTS
- Named to first Pro Bowl in 2008.
- Led the Titans with 16 passes defended and was third on the team with 109 tackles in 2007.
- Was third in the NFL in 2006 with 92 fumble-return yards.
- Drafted 215th overall from Samford University by the Tennesse Titans in 2006.

yard-churning machine for the Detroit Lions from 1989 to 1998. Yet watching how Finnegan defends against the run, one can't help but think the young Titans corner would love facing a legendary force like Sanders.

He was born Cortland Temujin Finnegan in Fayetteville, North Carolina, on February 2, 1984. He was raised by his mother, Linda, a single parent, and her 20-year career in the Army involved plenty of moving. From the ages of two to five, Finnegan was in Korea.

At Milton High School in Florida, Finnegan excelled offensively and defensively in football, and as a point guard in basketball. His four years at Samford were also decorated with

individual honors, including All-Ohio Valley Conference first-team selections in his final three years. A free safety at that stage of his career, Finnegan offered more by returning punts and kickoffs.

The Titans didn't rush Finnegan once he made the team in 2006, starting him twice (once at nickel back and once cornerback) in the 16 games he played. One of his highlights as a rookie occurred a week before Christmas when he recovered a fumble and returned it 92 yards for his first pro TD. It was the third-longest fumble return for a major in Titans history.

Finnegan started all 16 games in 2007 and continued to lay the groundwork as a defensive catalyst. He flourished at the start

of 2008 with two interceptions in Week 1 against Jacksonville, an interception in Week 2 at Cincinnati, followed by a 99-yard interception return for a touchdown in Week 3 against Houston.

His performance in 2008 put him into a head-to-head battle with Oakland's Nnamdi Asomugha in the Associated Press All-Pro voting. The final tabulation saw Asomugha, a first round draft choice, edge the seventh-rounder, 32–31. Considering the caliber of these two corners, this won't be the last time they'll battle for top honors at their position.

And don't expect Finnegan to tone down his play — the Titans like him just the way he is.

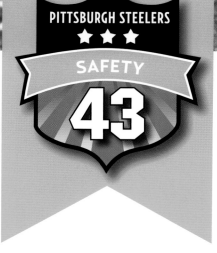

PITTSBURGH STEELERS
★ ★ ★
SAFETY
43

TROY POLAMALU

Safety Troy Polamalu is usually one of the most noticeable players whenever the Pittsburgh Steelers are on the field. Some might suggest the man wearing No. 43 in black and gold gets noticed because of his long hair, which according to one report has not been cut since the year 2000. In truth, it's his outstanding play that most consistently causes Polamalu to stand out. With a career-high seven interceptions, Polamalu

had one of his best years during the 2008 season and played an important role in getting his team to the Super Bowl. During the AFC championship game against the Baltimore Ravens, Polamalu was at his absolute best. First he stopped the Ravens on key fourth down gamble by timing a leap at the line of scrimmage and stuffing Baltimore quarterback Joe Flacco at the line. Later, with the contest still on the line and only

4:24 to play, Polamalu picked off Flacco and returned the ball 40 yards for a touchdown by darting all over the field like a running back might. The play nailed down a 23–14 win for the Steelers, who then beat Arizona to claim their sixth Super Bowl in franchise history.

The Steelers have developed a reputation for knowing exactly what kind of players they like, especially on defense. They were focused on Polamalu after he completed a stellar career at USC and moved up from 20th to 16th in the 2003 draft to select the 5-foot-10, 207-pound safety. It marked the first time Pittsburgh made a deal to move up in the draft and it was also the first occasion in which the team took a safety in the first round. That says a lot about how much the team coveted Polamalu.

Like many other players, Polamalu's NFL career started slowly and he earned his stripes on special teams as a rookie, although he did see some time in the defensive backfield. By the time the 2004 season began, Polamalu was deemed ready for starting action and he never looked back. His first full campaign saw him record 96 tackles and haul in

CAREER HIGHLIGHTS

- Ranked fourth in tackles in 2008 on the a Steelers team that possessed the best rated defense in the league.
- Five-time Pro Bowl selection (2004–2008).
- Drafted 16th overall from the University of Southern California by the Pittsburgh Steelers in 2003.
- Two-time All-American at USC.

five interceptions, but a loss in the AFC title game to New England meant a bad ending to an outstanding year. However, the hard-hitting Polamalu had learned a great deal about playing his position and made a tape of the best safeties in the league so he could study their moves and improve.

IN THE HUDDLE
Polamalu tied an NFL record for safeties by posting three sacks at Houston in Week 2 of the 2005 season.

Polamalu learned his lessons well and the Steeler coaching staff decided he was a special player, so — with some parameters in place — he was basically given free reign to do as he pleased on the field. He can lineup along the line of scrimmage or a little further back where a linebacker might be and, of course, in the traditional safety position. No matter what angle he takes, the opposition has to be aware of Polamalu because he is the most likely Steeler to make the tackle or breakup a play. He has enough speed and determination to roam all over the field and, when he hits, it's a serious wallop. The Steelers are able to

design their defensive system to deceive other teams and Polamalu's ability to breakup plays while seemingly coming from nowhere allows the defensive unit to be successful.

After a great regular season in 2005, Pittsburgh won the Super Bowl XL against Seattle with the defense holding the Seahawks to just 10 points. Three years later, the Steelers were back in the big game and Polamalu was given the task of trying to shutdown Arizona's star receiver, Larry Fitzgerald. For about three quarters, Polamalu did an outstanding job. But the fourth period

proved difficult. Fitzgerald got away from the tough Steeler coverage and gave his team a late lead with a touchdown reception after he took a pass across the middle of the field. It was one of the very few times Polamalu and some of his teammates could be seen chasing a receiver with no chance of making the tackle. The Steeler offense came back to score a late touchdown of their own to give Polamalu his second Super Bowl ring.

At the age of 27, Polamalu is still very much in his prime and if his performance in 2008 is any indication, the soft-spoken safety will be a force for years to come.

BALTIMORE RAVENS

SAFETY

20

ED REED

Ed Reed's 2008 season was in jeopardy even before it started because of chronic neck and shoulder problems. He took it easy during training camp, but was ready to go for the first game of the season at Cincinnati and did not miss a game the entire year. He worked closely with the Ravens trainers and went to see his doctor every Friday to keep himself prepared for each week's game. Not only did he suit up for all 16 contests, Reed was simply outstanding, earning himself a spot on the Pro Bowl starting lineup. Not bad for a player many thought would have to sit out the year or maybe even retire.

By the time the 2008 season was over, Reed led the NFL with nine interceptions and was a serious candidate to be named the league's best defensive player. Although that recognition went to Pittsburgh's James Harrison, the 30-year-old certainly left his mark on the season and the NFL record book. His biggest plays of the season were a score on a 22-yard fumble versus Washington after stripping the ball away from Redskins running back Clinton Portis and two interceptions in the Ravens' playoff win at Miami — one for a touchdown. He rewrote the NFL record for the longest interception return when he returned for 107 yards against Philadelphia, breaking the previous mark of 106 yards that he set in 2004.

IN THE HUDDLE

Reed is the active leader in the NFL with 1,144 interception-return yards. He is sixth on the all-time list.

There is no player Reed cannot cover and he roams from sideline-to-sideline to get to the football. If the ball is in the air, you can bet Reed has a chance to grab it. He relishes the opportunity to turn his ball-hawking skills into points by taking a pass back to the oppositions' end zone. He is also very disciplined and in position to make a play on just about every snap.

Titans quarterback Kerry Collins paid the ultimate compliment to Reed by saying any quarterback has

to be aware of where he is at all times. The veteran safety takes great pride in preparing himself for every opponent. Reed watches more game tape than any other player and that helps him read plays with incredible intuition. He shares observations with teammates and coaches, and that helped the Ravens develop one of the stingiest and most feared defenses in the entire NFL. Reed embraced the role of being a veteran who was asked to tutor some of Baltimore's younger players. Both Reed and Ravens coach John Harbaugh agreed the current competitive state of the NFL means team work is an absolute must for any club to achieve success. Reed's attitude certainly went a long way in helping the Ravens make a smooth transition from former coach Brian Billick to Harbaugh in 2008. The transition went so well that the Ravens made it all the way

to the AFC championship, where they lost to the eventual Super Bowl champion Pittsburgh Steelers.

The Ravens were fortunate to get Reed with the 24th pick of the 2002 NFL draft after he had earned All-American honors while attending the University of Miami. The 5-foot-11, 200-pounder earned a scholarship to the school by lifting his academic standing after he moved out of his parents' house (with their approval) and began to focus his efforts on getting an education. On the field, Reed upset his college coaches by intercepting passes in practice. The coaches thought that would ruin the confidence of the quarterbacks, but Reed knew playing like he would in a game was the best way to prepare. By 2004, he was named defensive player of the year in the NFL — only the third safety to earn that distinction.

CAREER HIGHLIGHTS

- 2004 NFL defensive player of the year.
- Five-time Pro Bowl selection (2003, 2004, 2006–2008)
- Posted nine interceptions in 2004 and 2008 to lead the NFL both times.
- Led the NFL in non-offensive touchdowns in 2008 with three.

The Ravens lost defensive coordinator Rex Ryan to the New York Jets after the 2008 season, but Reed will do everything he can to prepare his team no matter who is calling the plays. He will be a heart-and-soul leader for Baltimore and you can bet he'll always be standing in the right place to make a big play.

GREEN BAY PACKERS
CORNERBACK 21

CHARLES WOODSON

Cornerback Charles Woodson was not especially interested in playing for the Green Bay Packers. He did sign a lucrative seven-year free agent contract worth $52.7 million with the Packers prior to the start of the 2006 season, but his preference would have been to play for one of the Florida-based teams. However, the reality was only the Packers showed interest in Woodson, who was almost 30 years old and coming off a season that saw him miss 10 games with a broken leg. In addition, he was not exactly seen in a good light for his attitude and approach, so he might have been fortunate to get any offers at all. Woodson could have stayed home and waited for the phone to ring, but he wanted to continue his career. It was not an easy transition to Green Bay for Woodson, who did not see eye-to-eye with the Packer coaches early on. He was fined on more than one occasion and he battled with head coach Mike McCarthy, but he was determined to see if his situation would improve. Soon enough Woodson began to win over his coaches, teammates and the devoted Packer fans with his outstanding play.

IN THE HUDDLE
Woodson's six career interception returns for touchdown ranks him sixth among active players and 13th all time.

Woodson seemed destined for stardom in the NFL after a great college career at the University of Michigan. He became a starter for the Wolverines in his freshman year and by his junior year in 1997, he was in the running for the Heisman Trophy. Woodson was part of a great team that had an undefeated season and gained a share of the national championship. He won all kinds awards for his great play, including being named the best defensive player in college, and became the third Michigan player to take the Heisman. It also marked the first time that a defense-only player was named winner of the prestigious award. His great play caught the attention of the professional scouts and he declared himself eligible for the NFL draft

after his junior year. The Oakland Raiders were thrilled to select him fourth overall in the 1998 draft. He started in all 16 games as a rookie with the Raiders and recorded five interceptions, returning one for a touchdown. Woodson was a perennial Pro Bowl player during his time with the Raiders and recorded one interception when Tampa Bay defeated Oakland 48–21 in Super Bowl XXXVII.

The Raiders faltered badly in the 2003 season, posting a 4–12 mark, and Woodson fell out of favor with coach Bill Callahan. Even though he was not content with his situation, Woodson stayed with the Raiders for the next two seasons. It was a tough time for one of the highest-paid defensive players in the league as he endured broken legs on two occasions. Talk began that Woodson had lost a step, that his interest in playing was on the decline and that he was now an injury-prone performer. He was clearly through with the Raiders

by the end of the 2005 season and the Packers made headlines when they signed Woodson and gave him $10.5 million in the first year of the deal. Woodson regained his form in 2006 when he picked off a career-high eight passes — one going all the way back for a touchdown — and he managed to play in all 16 games despite nagging injuries to his knee and shoulder. It also turned out Green Bay was not nearly as hard a place to play as Woodson had imagined and heard from people. He started to enjoy being a Packer and came to appreciate the unique fans of the fabled Green and Gold.

Woodson had a good season in 2007 recording four interceptions in 14 games for a 13–3 team, but the Packers lost the NFC championship game to the New York Giants. He was even better in 2008 — despite a very painful toe injury suffered early in the season — and he was named to the Pro Bowl once again. He rarely

CAREER HIGHLIGHTS

- Named the 1998 NFL defensive rookie of the year.
- Selected to five Pro Bowls (1998–2001, 2008).
- Posted a career-high eight interceptions and 26 passes defended in 2006.
- Drafted fourth overall from the University of Michigan by the Oakland Raiders in 1998.

practiced during the 2008 campaign, but he was ready to play every week and picked off seven passes, second-most in the NFL. Woodson has the ability to make quarterbacks believe their man is open when in fact he is lurking in the shadows, waiting to jump on any opportunity to make a key interception. That skill is one of many that make Woodson such an effective NFLer.

Acknowledgments

The authors would like to acknowledge the following media sources used to compile the profiles in this book:

12th Man Magazine; 2008 NFL Record and Fact Book; Atlanta Journal-Constitution; Austin American-Statesman; Baltimore Sun; Baseball Prospectus; Beckett Fantasy Football; Boston Globe; Buffalo News; CarolinaGrowl.com; CBS Sports; Charlotte Observer; Chicago Tribune; Cleveland Leader; CNNSI.com; Cooley Zone; Dallas Morning News; Dallas News; DC Sports Pulse; demarcusware94.com; Denver Post; Detroit Free Press; Eagle-Tribune; Encyclopedia of World Biography; Epilepsy Foundation of America; ESPN; Fantasy Football Draft Book; Fort Worth Star-Telegram FOX Sports; Globe and Mail; Green Bay Press Gazette; Honolulu Advertiser; Honolulu Star-Bulletin; Houston Chronicle; HuskerExtra; jeffgarcia.com; jockbio.com; Kansas City Star; Louisiana Daily News; mattforte.com; Miami Herald; Milwaukee Wisconsin Journal Sentinel; Minneapolis-St. Paul Star Tribune; National Post; NationMaster.com NBC Sports; New York Daily News; New York Post; New York Times; Newsday; Newsobserver.com; NFL Football Online Betting; NFL Teams Official Websites; Notredame.com; Oakland Tribune; Palm Beach Post; Patriots Football Weekly; People Magazine; Philadelphia Courier-Post; Philadelphia Daily News; Philadelphia Inquirer; Pittsburgh Post-Gazette; Pittsburgh Tribune; Pro Football Weekly; Prosportsdaily.com; San Diego Union-Tribune; San Francisco Chronicle; South Florida Sun-Sentinel; Sporting News; Sports Illustrated; St. Louis Post-Dispatch; StarTribune.com; The Huddle; The Progress-Index; The Starting Five; The Tennessean; tonyromo9.com; Toronto Star; Toronto Sun; TransWorldNews; USA Today; Washington Post; Yahoo! Sports

PROFILE INDEX